DEAR THE MAN UPSTAIRS

DEAR
THE MAN
UPSTAIRS

MAYTAL BOOTH

NEW DEGREE PRESS

COPYRIGHT © 2021 MAYTAL BOOTH

DEAR THE MAN UPSTAIRS

ISBN

978-1-63730-317-7   *Paperback*

978-1-63730-318-4   *Kindle Ebook*

978-1-63730-319-1   *Digital Ebook*

This book is dedicated to Naomi Booth. It's been a crazy twenty years, and I couldn't have made it this far without you.

CONTENTS

———

AUTHOR'S NOTE

———

Dear Readers,

When I first started writing *Dear the Man Upstairs*, I did not know it would become a book. I was sitting in a creative writing class, sixteen years old, drafting a single narrative letter because that was what my teacher had told me to do.

I thought about who my classmates would choose as the recipients of their letters. I thought maybe they would write to a classmate, a lover (always a lover when you're a teenager), a friend, maybe an enemy. I, like every sixteen-year-old, wanted to be *different*. I wanted to be totally outlandish and yet safely secured away from ridiculous.

So I thought to myself, *Who is the most out-there person someone could write a letter to? Who will no one else think to have as their recipient?*

The answer came in a startling epiphany—God.

I grew up in a religious Jewish household. My father is a Rabbi, and my mother is an educator of Judaism. God and related questions are often at the forefront of my mind, which is why I thought of a divine power so quickly as a recipient for my letter.

Once I had *who was being written to,* I needed to find out *who was writing.* As a child, I struggled with the many euphemisms for God. It was inconceivable to me that one being had so many names.

So, in one way to be a bit funny, and in another way to make the work not explicitly religious, I decided that the writer of the letter was a child. She addressed the letter to "the Man Upstairs," unaware of what exactly the name represented. It was just someone she'd heard her grandmother talk about a lot.

The letter started to take form then. She's a fourth grader (a grade I remember clearly), a bit different (she gets scared of loud noises easily, like I did back in the day), and she's so unapologetically vibrant the people around her sometimes need to shield their eyes.

She's curious in that first letter, asking questions to a stranger and hoping someone can make order of her chaotic world. When I shared it in class, my seatmate said, "You have to write more."

So, I kept writing and writing. I thought about what people often consider to be an ideal child: an extroverted, athletic, intelligent, empathetic, disciplined, and obedient angel. (No one really has children like this.)

My main character, in her own ways, has these attributes. She's friendly, bright, and loves the people in her life. She is athletic, and she has discipline when it suits her. She also has a hard time sitting still, dealing with things that are uncomfortable for her, and understanding social norms. She sees a psychologist to help her develop strategies for a challenging world. She is hard to be around sometimes. Even if she is not what many people would consider an "ideal child," she is still happy and healthy.

After I wrote a few letters, someone wrote my main character back.

The genre of this epistolary novel is young adult, but truthfully, I believe it has broad appeal to anyone in a family. Mothers, daughters, fathers, grandfathers, and especially grandmothers will see themselves in some of the characters. Growing up, my family read each other books like the *Penderwicks* and *Nuclear Family,* both of which influenced my writing style for this novel.

I grew up with heartwarming books forming the backbone of many night cuddle-sessions and Friday afternoon family times. It felt very natural to write my own read-aloud friendly novel. It's practically my tradition.

My main character's family is in some ways modeled off of my own, and in some ways she is very different from me. She is Christian, a religion I do not practice. My mother, however, converted to Judaism from Christianity. Jewish households are wonderful places, but they can be loud and abrasive. Private hurts become public accusations in a matter of minutes.

Members of my mother's side of the family, by contrast, are a lot more careful in how they express discomfort. There's a culture of keeping things to yourself and rarely voicing (explicitly) the source of contention. Her family is far better than my father's at the art of passive aggression.

This dynamic is integral to my main character's family life. Her grandmother and mother do not get along in the slightest. The mother and daughter-in-law pair talk to each other almost exclusively in hidden barbs and pointed criticisms. My main character, being the socially oblivious individual she is, misses the tenseness of these interactions and only understands something is wrong during obvious fights.

This book is a coming-of-age novel, but it is not only about my main character growing up. It is a story about a family growing apart and together and wiser and melancholy. It is about expectations and how breaking them can sometimes be frustrating and beautiful in equal measure.

Dear the Man Upstairs will always carry a piece of me, sixteen years old and writing in a humid classroom full of sweaty teens. I didn't know from the first letter, or even the fifth, that I was writing a book. Sometimes it still surprises me that these letters became a complete novel.

This has been the journey of a lifetime. Thank you, dear readers, for coming on it with me.

Yours,
Maytal Booth

PART I

EGG

Dear the Man Upstairs,

Who are you, and is "the Man Upstairs" even your real name? That's a nickname, right? I bet your real name is John, David, Kevin, or something. I know a lot of Johns. My grandma and you must be really good friends because she talks about you a lot, and she doesn't really talk about anyone because she doesn't like most people and "gossiping is bad." Do you talk about her a lot? Does she talk about me a lot? Do you also not have a lot of friends? I have two and a half. I'm writing to you because I think we should be friends. I don't have any friends who are adults, and I think adults probably need friends as much as kids need them.

I asked my grandma once why it rained, and she said it rains whenever you want it to or when you are crying. I think you've been crying a lot lately, because the sky has so many clouds, the trees keep dripping water, and the puddles are getting bigger. Are you okay? I hope you're not too sad.

Maybe you just really like the way rain looks. I don't. If you really do control rain, could you make it stop? I do like rainbows. You can't get rainbows without rain. Wait, would you be able to do that? You totally should. That would be so cool.

Mommy says I get distracted too easily, so I might get off topic sometimes, and I'm sorry. I asked her why I can't focus like the other kids, and why I get scared at the sound of people on the second floor above my classroom and then need to hide under my desk even though my friends (well, not my friends *yet*, but people who might be friends if I try a little harder) will laugh, and she said it's because you have a plan. Do you have a plan? I feel like my life is a little unfair because my teacher, Mrs. N, is always mad at me for running around and getting off topic. I would really like to know why I am the way I am. Daddy says what doesn't kill me makes me stronger, but all I have are bruises on the fronts of my knees from falling out of the tree in the schoolyard.

Why are bruises blue and black? I asked my mommy, and she said to bother someone else, so then I asked my grandma, and she was reading but she said because *you* said so, but somehow I think there's a better answer. Anyways, we haven't met yet, but Grandma Jen says I need to trust you. This is confusing because Mommy always tells me not to trust strangers, which you are. Grandma Jen tells me Mommy is overprotective and distant and so I should not listen to her.

Please write me back, Man Upstairs. What does it even mean, upstairs? We're on the top floor of our apartment building, and people can't go on to the roof. At least, I can't. Do you live on the roof? That would be super weird and a little dangerous. Be careful and please write back to me. I really want a pen pal.

Sincerely,

Miss W (Mommy says that it's bad to tell strangers your *full* name, so I'm only giving you the first letter of my last name.)

Dear the Man Upstairs,

You haven't yet responded to my first letter. Do you have any paper or pencils? Just in case you don't, I'll put some pencils in the envelope with this letter. I hate mechanical pencils, so I hope you don't mind regular yellow ones. Maybe you won't need any pencils, anyway, because you've probably already written me back, and it's just that the mail is taking forever because of all the storms. Are you okay? You're not crying too much, are you? Mommy and I cry all the time, but I don't think I've ever seen Grandma Jen or Daddy cry.

Grandma Jen says you're called "the Man Upstairs" because you live in the sky. Does that mean that somewhere there's a staircase that goes all the way into the clouds? Can you tell me where it is? Actually, maybe you shouldn't tell me because I might get lost trying to find it. I get lost a lot, and sometimes it's just in the grocery store. The other day, Mommy brought me to help her buy some things for dinner. I needed to use the restroom except I accidentally went to the storeroom, and there were all these cardboard boxes, and I couldn't find my way out.

The store had to go into lockdown because everyone thought maybe someone had taken me when Mommy couldn't find me. I could hear people looking for me on the intercom, but I wasn't sure where to go. I think I went the wrong direction because I ended up by a wall, and then an employee found me and had to tell everyone I was okay on the intercom. And Mommy was really mad at me when I found her again. So maybe don't tell me about where the staircase is because I could end up on the wrong side of the sky, and I don't think clouds have intercoms.

The staircase you live above must be really long. I don't think I could walk up that many flights of stairs. I get out of breath walking up the six flights of stairs to our apartment when the power's out like it was yesterday.

Do you walk up the super huge flight of stairs every day, or do you just stay in the sky most of the time? I think I would stay in the sky if I could because then I'd never have to go to the doctor's. I have to go tomorrow because my teacher, Mrs. N (we call her Mrs. N because her full last name is NyQuil-al-oe-vera-phobia or something), said I should go to a doctor for some testing. My mommy was really upset at her and yelled for a long time, and then I was taken outside by Mrs. Casey, the yard teacher, and the principal came and talked with Mommy while I got to use the swing set. And now I have an appointment with someone named Dr. Keaty.

I don't think that the doctor will learn anything about me. I'm just a normal girl who does normal girl things. It's not like I'm sick or anything. I don't want to get tested because I hate tests, but I like doctors. Daddy's a doctor, but he works at the county clinic, and he's trying to move into something called "development" at a "for-profit institution" so he can "finally make some gosh darn money with the degree." That means he's trying to be the person who asks the government or rich people for money, I think. He doesn't like being a doctor at the clinic very much.

Please write back to me.

Sincerely,

Miss W

Dear the Man Upstairs,

I checked all our mail yesterday, and there was nothing addressed to me except one letter, but Mommy took it from me before I could open it. I think it was your letter to me, and even though Mommy didn't let me read it, thanks for writing! It looked like it was typed, which makes sense because I wouldn't want to use yellow pencils if I could avoid them even though I was the one who sent you them. I don't know if it's because the school bus is yellow or Mommy's yucky vitamins are yellow or Grandma Jen's stupid bag is yellow, but I think yellow is an ugly color.

I asked Mommy for green pencils, but she said they don't exist. Well, Mommy once said aliens didn't exist, but Mrs. N told me today that Mars had (or maybe still has) water and maybe even tiny little aliens smaller than my eyes or maybe smaller than my eyes can see. I'm not really sure. The point is that things Mommy says don't exist sometimes *do* exist, and I'm going to find green pencils someday. Probably pretty soon, too, because Grandma Jen says that Mommy doesn't get me green pencils because she's lazy and not because they don't exist.

I asked Mommy about the letter, and I think she lied to me. She said it was just my test results from the other day when we went to see Dr. Keaty.

I don't like tests very much because sometimes (most times) I have a hard time sitting still until the end, and Mrs. N gets a little upset with me for being "distracting." Like this one time, we were doing a math test, and I was really bored, so I started drumming the "Imperial March" from *Star Wars* because I had watched it the night before with Daddy, even though Mommy says that "TV will rot my brain." I was just drumming it on the desk, but then I started getting really into it, and I began humming it. So I'm at my desk going, "bum bum bum" and so on for the whole first part of the melody. Then I get to the refrain, and I just start belting out the song, and then Mrs. N told me, "Stop it right now. You're distracting the other students."

So then I just drummed the song on my desk for about fifteen seconds, and then Mrs. N sent me outside of the classroom. Tests and I are *not* friends.

This test wasn't so bad, though. Mommy and I drove to the office, and we went down a hallway with purple walls and green polka dots. The lady behind the counter talked to me like I was a baby. When I said I liked the green polka dots because I have green eyes and me and the decoration matched, she said in this high-pitched cooing voice, "You do match!" and offered me a sugar-free purple lollipop. I did not like the way the lady behind the desk was talking to me because I am *nine* and not a toddler, but I do like lollipops. I went to take the lollipop, but Mommy pushed my hand down and said I didn't need any candy, so I didn't end up getting to eat it after all.

Then we went back into Dr. Keaty's room, which had *Doctor Keaty* written on a board on the front of the door. I think it would be cool if one day I have an office with my name on the front. When we went inside, there was this kind of tan couch and then a large desk. Dr. Keaty had dark skin and dark hair in a bun, and she had these deep brown eyes that looked like they were staring straight into my soul and *judging* me.

The doctor asked me some questions. They were all not scary at all and a bunch easier than the real tests I have to do at school on spelling and fast multiplication.

"Do you get up from your seat a lot at school?" she asked.

"Yes," I answered. "I have to get up to go to the bathroom or to take a break from working sometimes or to find whatever I dropped or to see what's outside the window. Everyone gets out of their seat sometimes."

"Do you have trouble playing quietly?"

"No," I said. "It's just sometimes I have to remember to use my inside voice."

"Do you have trouble wearing jeans?"

That one was a good one because yes, I do. Jeans have the seam that just *itches* for no reason, and I can't stand them even if Mommy always says I would look so darling in them instead of the pajama pants I choose to wear. Daddy gets mad at her sometimes when she tries to make me wear scratchy dresses and pinching shoes. Sometimes I have to wear fancy dresses, anyway, and then I'll pull on their tags until they rip, and Mommy gets mad at me, but then I get to change.

Anyway, Dr. Keaty asked a few more questions like those, and then she gave me some cars to play with and talked to Mommy. And Mommy said that the letter she wouldn't let me see was the "results" but all I did was answer questions, so I don't know what the doctor could have found. Mommy said we'd have to go in again, though, and that I had to start seeing Dr. Keaty twice a week. Talking with Dr. Keaty isn't so bad, but I don't think the two of us are going to be friends, not like you and me might be friends one day. She's very professional and never talks about herself. I don't think I've ever had an adult talk to me *about* me for so long ever before. I've talked to Dr. Keaty three times now. In our first time together, she suggested to Mommy that it might be good to prescribe me some medications, but Mommy said, "No."

Dr. Keaty said that was fine, and now we just talk to each other. I can't tell if I like her or not.

But enough about me. How are you? Mommy says I talk about myself too much. She says I need to start letting people talk about themselves a little, otherwise just hearing me talk will be boring. I asked her, "What is it like being old?" after she told me this, but she got angry. Since she always complains to Daddy about how she looks wrinkly, I thought this would be a good thing to ask. It wasn't because Mommy got snappy with me and said I should never ask someone that. I thought she was being a bit rude.

I talked to Daddy about it later, and he told me that I should never ask a lady what her age is and that I should always say they look younger than they do. I think tomorrow I'll tell Mrs. N, who I think is about one hundred seven, that she looks thirty-one and a half. Maybe then she'll be more okay with me hiding under my desk. Mrs. N doesn't like it when I go to play with blocks when she's talking, so I've been working with Dr. Keaty to sit more still in my seat. I have this game I play with Dr. Keaty and Mommy. If I sit in my seat, I can wiggle my hands and go through tensing every bit of my body, from my toes to my head (but I don't know how to tense my hair). If at the end of the day, I didn't get out of my seat once except for the bathroom and lunch, Mrs. N tells Mommy, and Mommy gives me a sticker on a chart. I told Dr. Keaty that my favorite candy is Snickers, and she said she'll give me one if I ever get five weeks with all stickers. I'll let you know when I get there.

Warmly,

Miss W

PS

I am working with Dr. Keaty who is a "how kids grow" mind doctor to help me out with the world. Apparently, I'm not only overly energetic but also not the best with people skills, so she's helping me figure "social cues" out. In this last session, we looked at a lot of faces, and I had to guess if they were angry or sad or something. I thought they all looked hungry, but that's probably because we'd spent the whole time talking about Snickers.

Dear the Man Upstairs,

Hello! I hope you are having a good weekend even though it's been raining a lot. Even if it's raining because you're sad (I really hope that's not why!), I kind of like the rain because Daddy always says I am the best puddle splasher in all the

Midwest. At school, there are always slugs right after it rains, and they look kind of funny.

There's this boy in my class named Stupid Sean Hanner, who I've known since I was two because our dads are friends, and he's been annoying the whole time I've known him. He bit me once when I was four. Stupid Sean Hanner doesn't like slugs, and he always freaks out whenever I pick one up and wiggle it in front of his face. I think if it was anyone else, I might feel bad about making them freak out, but Stupid Sean Hanner doesn't like me and I don't like *him*, so I don't feel that bad about scaring him a little once in a while. Plus, I used to be taller than him when we were little, but now he's taller than me, so I think that's unfair.

Rain also brings mushrooms, and me and my best friend Nina build castles out of the mushrooms, sticks, and leaves in the schoolyard. Stupid Sean Hanner sometimes steps on our castles with his stupid sneakers, but yesterday, I put a slug on his arm after he ruined my castle. I think that should keep him from going around and destroying my masterpieces for a little bit.

Today in class, we learned all about bees. I've decided that when I grow up, I'm going to be one. Bees are better than people; that's what I think. Did you know that in beehives, the women hold all the power? The guys get pushed out every winter. I think it would be super fun if next time Stupid Sean Hanner annoyed me, I could remind him that I was the boss just because I was a girl.

I told Daddy all about bees and the power of women, and he said, "You go ahead and shatter the glass ceiling, sweetheart," and then wandered away to have a phone call. I asked Mommy what the "glass ceiling" was, and she said that for a long time, women would be able to see what it would be like to be rich, but they couldn't get there. Bees don't even have money, so I don't know how I would be able to shatter the glass ceiling, and broken glass is dangerous, but Daddy doesn't often talk in ways I can understand.

That's okay, though, because I was thinking about bees. The queen bee has all this power, and the workers just bring her stuff, and all she has to do is lay eggs. And then I realized: Mommy is kind of like a queen bee. Her job is to take care of me, and Daddy just brings her stuff, like jewelry and credit cards, and she doesn't do much else. I don't want to be like Mommy, though. I really hope I can grow up into a real bee with six legs and wings and everything.

Daddy was actually complaining a few days ago when he thought I was sleeping. He said that now that I'm older, Mommy should go back to work. He was saying she could do something part-time. Mommy said something about me being a full-time job. I suppose I am. I mean, Mommy is my mommy all the time, but I think Daddy is, too, so I wonder what she meant. Anyways, when we were watching this video on bees, we learned they do a dance to tell other bees where the flowers are. I've decided I'm going to learn to dance because that's the first step toward becoming a bee. Thanks for letting me talk so much about myself.

Warmly,

Miss W

PS

Both Nina *and* Stupid Sean Hanner have smartphones so I asked Mommy if I could have a smartphone too. She said I needed to be smart first. Well, I am smart. Daddy and Dr. Keaty say so. Even Mrs. N said it's too bad I have a difficult time because otherwise, I'd be a bone-if-fried genius. You think I'm smart, don't you?

Dear Miss W,

Thank you for all your letters. I have many friends, including your grandmother and even your Mrs. N, but I'm hoping you and I can be friends too. Activity isn't a bad thing at all. Plenty of geniuses have to move around a little, and sometimes creativity is best expressed through movement. I myself move all the time, from place to place, to be with people a little here and a little there. Staying in one place all the time just doesn't suit me. There is no reason it should suit you.

Sincerely,
the Man Upstairs

Dear the Man Upstairs,

You want to be my friend? That would be AMAZING. Yes! I think one day I'll learn how to be a bit less active, even if that's something you like to be. All the adults tell me that being "hyperactive" isn't a good thing, even though they tell me on TV that I need my sixty minutes a day of being active. Mommy explained that TV people and real people are not the same, but she also said that the same guy who told me to move around more was right when he told me to wash my hands for at least twenty seconds.

I asked her why he was only right half of the time, and she said most people are right only half of the time. Then I asked her if she was right only half of the time, and if maybe she was wrong about that number. She got really mad and told me that no, she is right all of the time, and only other people are wrong. I asked her if Daddy was wrong a lot like most people, and she said maybe. So then I asked what about Grandma Jen because I know Grandma Jen is super smart, and Mommy said, "Yes, absolutely your grandmother is wrong half of the time. Maybe even seventy-five percent of the time."

Now I need to talk to Grandma Jen because she doesn't realize how often she's been wrong.

I really want to become a bee. I begged and begged Mommy to let me take dance classes. You know bees talk to each other by dancing. I will need to know how to dance when I become a bee so that I can eat. Mommy talked to Dr. Keaty, who said it could be good to "give me an avenue to express my energy in a productive manner," and then Mommy finally let me join a ballet class. At first, I thought that this was a bad idea, because it's not like bees dance *ballet*, but then Teacher Lara said that ballet is the foundation for every kind of dance other than hip-hop and if you master ballet, you can master anything. Because of that, I was happy to be in the class.

And guess who else is in my ballet class? Nina! She's one of my two best friends. Well, she's not in my class, she's actually the level above me, but Teacher Lara said that if I work extra hard this year, I'll be moved up to Nina's level next year. I'm working super hard.

I was in Social Studies class, and we were learning about the Potawatomi tribe when I realized, *I could spend this time practicing dancing!* Well, then my mind just went immediately to this like place where all I could think about was the fact that I could be dancing, and then I realized all at once, *but I'm not dancing right now.*

I did the only logical thing. I started practicing my high kicks and used the desk as a kind of ballet barre. But that was kind of a small bit of practice, so then I started practicing my split jumps. Nina gave me a thumbs up from her desk. Little Yvette Guiteau, the shortest girl in our class who always wears her hair in two blond pigtails, rolled her eyes and raised her hand and said, "Mrs. N, *someone* is being distracting again."

Mrs. N sighed, and it looked to me like she'd been trying to pretend that I wasn't dancing so that way she wouldn't have to say anything, but then she said, "Miss W, I need you to stop jumping and go back to your desk."

But I was on the path to becoming a bee, and I was not about to let something like school stop me. "Mrs. N," I tried to explain, "dancing is how bees find food and—"

"Yes, I understand that," Mrs. N said, "but you are in a classroom. I know that you've been working on strategies. I need you to control your impulses and sit down. Please."

I said, "But I'm just—"

And then Mrs. N yelled, "There is no *just!* You need to listen to me." She took a deep breath. "I need you to go outside for a little while to cool down, okay?"

And I said, "Yes, Mrs. N." I was really happy to go out into the hallway because it has blue carpets, and it's really soft so it's easy to jump. I started cartwheeling and doing split jumps and the whole thing, and Nina and the rest of the class were watching me clearly through the little window on our classroom door.

Then Mrs. N made eye contact with me, and she came out and said, "You need to go to the office right now. Right now."

I felt my eyes stinging a bit as I walked down the hall. The office sent me to the school counselor who works in one of the portables. The room smelled like old tuna. The counselor was wearing too much lipstick. The room was kind of bright. The counselor saw that I have a medical record on file and asked me, "Did you forget to take your medication?"

I said, "I don't have any medication."

She called my mommy and asked if I was medicated, and then she got off the phone and told me, "You should think about getting a prescription to help you." I didn't even go back to class.

Mommy picked me up, and she was super angry. When we were driving home, she pulled over on the side of the road, the one that's two streets away from home and has all the bushes. She said, "There is *nothing* wrong with you, okay?"

And I said, "Okay," because I feel like I am a fun girl.

"But you need to focus, okay? Because the people at your school don't know that there is nothing wrong with you. They get worried. And I need you to get it together because you don't need medications. You can fix this, okay? That's on you." Mommy was freaking me out a bit.

"Yes, Mommy. Of course."

Then Mommy pulled out the little chart with all the stickers that shows my progress for sitting still in class—you know, the one that we give to Dr. Keaty to see if I can get a Snickers—and she tore off every single one even though it ripped the paper. Then she looked down at the ripped paper, and looked at me, and then unbuckled my seatbelt and pulled me in for the tightest hug I've ever had.

"You're okay," she said. "You're okay, you're okay, you're okay."

I was okay, but it felt like maybe Mommy wasn't. What do you think?

Sincerely,

Miss W

PS

Halloween is coming up, and I think I'll be a crayon because dressing up as a bee would just prove that I'm not a real one. Also, I wonder what it's like to be a crayon. I don't think I'd like it. Nathan chews on all our class crayons, and then I never want to use them. Nina has a crush on Nathan, but I don't think it will last once she notices he likes to eat crayons. Do you like crayons? You wrote your letter in green pen, so maybe not. Maybe you'll like it better if I write to you in pen. I'll do that next.

Dear Miss W,
I can read your letters no matter how you write them. Pens and crayons are both mediums for you to express your beautiful thoughts. I do not think there is anything wrong with wanting to fit in or daring to be different. What matters is that you feel comfortable with yourself and do not change to please others. You only need to feel proud of the person you are; other people do not determine your value.
I can see that your mother and your teachers are strict, and that has challenges. Your teachers have to work hard at making a classroom that welcomes every student. Your mother is navigating a world that is different from the world she thought she would live in. Even so, she loves you. She is scared right now because this aspect of caring for you is new to her, and she wants the best for you. One day, it is my belief you will look back at these moments and remember all the love your mother gave you. Think positively, Miss W. A few kind thoughts will go a long way.
Fondly,
the Man Upstairs

Dear the Man Upstairs,
You wrote me back again! Thanks. I always try to think positively. Daddy says time passes faster when you're having fun, and I want to become a bee as fast as possible, so I try not to let myself be sad too often. Dr. Keaty tells me it's okay to be sad sometimes, but I'm not sure I believe her. Just like

you said, positivity goes a long way, right? And anyway, I see what you're saying about being nicer to Mommy and that she's trying hard and everything, but you don't live with her. It's easy to be nice and thoughtful to someone you haven't met.

For example, a few nights ago, my room was a little dirty, and Mommy only tripped twice on dirty socks and Mr. Wiggles, my stuffed teddy bear, who was chilling on the red carpet by my bed when she came in to kiss me goodnight. The next morning, she made me clean it all up even though it was the *weekend*. Daddy and I had just come back from church with Grandma Jen (we went to be nice to her) and Mommy put out a tray of cookies for Grandma Jen, which she *never* does because cookies are a "no-no" food, and then I couldn't even eat *one* single cookie.

Mommy told me to go clean up my room "for the love of all that is holy, *now*, or else there will be consequences." She scared me, so I went to go put my dirty clothing in the hamper and my three favorite toys (two cars and one stuffed bee) back in their bins and Mr. Wiggles back on the bed. I took little breaks during what I've decided to call the "Great Room Cleanup of Last Sunday," but every time I walked the five steps out into our living room to grab a cookie, Mommy sent me back to my room. I asked her, "Can I please have a cookie, just one cookie, Mommy, because I know they are sometimes snacks and maybe today could be sometimes?"

Mommy said, "I think I told you to clean up your room. We are not having this conversation until that floor is spotless."

It took me a whole forty-five minutes to sort through the layers of dirty clothes to have a clean room, and that was time I was going to spend having Grandma Jen tell me stories about Grandpa Claude. I mean, it's a good thing my room is clean now, so I guess it wasn't *all* bad, but when I finally did finish cleaning up my room, Mommy had already put away all the cookies and said that I could have some tomorrow after I finish all my homework. (This was a lie. I did my homework, and the cookie never happened.) Mommy looks out for me, but sometimes it feels like she goes about it the wrong way. ONE cookie wouldn't have killed anyone, least of all me. (Bees don't eat cookies, though, so I decided it was training for my life as an insect because otherwise, I might have cried.)

Fortunately, even if I didn't get a cookie, Grandma Jen told me a story about Grandpa Claude. I already knew this one. Grandpa Claude was the kind of kid (and adult) who didn't always think things through. He had an older sister (Aunt Catherine, but she's in an elderly home, and I've never met her) and when he was seven and she was fifteen, he asked her during a cold Illinois winter if his tongue would really stick to a metal pole if he licked it.

She said, "Yes."

He asked, "But would it really?"

She said, "Yes, Claude, I said it would."

But because Grandpa Claude was kind of like me, he licked this metal pole with a street sign by his house, and then he got stuck. His sister had to run up their porch and grab a warm towel. Apparently, she was really nice and didn't make fun of him at all, just slowly helped him peel his tongue back.

And Grandma Jen always says, "That was the first of your grandfather's many great adventures." Sometimes, like this last time she told it, she'll pull me onto her lap (well, most of me at any rate, I'm bigger now than when I fit all the way) and say, "I imagine you'll have great adventures of your own someday too."

And you know what? I'm sure I will. I'm gonna have to go on many adventures if I ever want to become a bee. Or become someone like Grandpa Claude. Either is good with me.

Warmly,

Miss W

PS

I learned something shocking today! My mommy is pregnant. It means she has a baby growing in her stomach, like how apples grow on trees except the baby is growing inside her. Mommy was pregnant when I was six. I asked her back then how she was watering the baby, and Mommy said that by drinking water and eating food, the baby will grow big and strong. Mommy watered the almond trees she tried to plant last spring, but she said they didn't grow because of "the gosh-darn Milwaukee climate." I hope that this new baby will grow.

Dear the Man Upstairs,

How are you? Yesterday, I had a slightly sad moment in my life. I realized two huge things, one: sometimes the Tooth Fairy forgets to give you anything, and two, it's going to be another seven months before I'm a big sister.

I'll start with the first tragedy. I'm a nine-year-old girl, and I am super mature and everything, but I don't lose a tooth every day. When I lose a tooth, I have some expectations. Mommy and I always write a note to the Tooth Fairy and leave her bottle caps full of milk and cheese in case she needs a snack. In the morning, the bottle caps are always empty, the note is gone, and the Tooth Fairy leaves me a letter. I always leave my tooth underneath my pillow, and the Tooth Fairy always takes it and leaves me a Snickers under my pillow. These are my Tooth Fairy visit expectations.

None of this happened last night. I mean, I wrote the Tooth Fairy note and left out the capfuls and put the tooth under my pillow, but in the morning, everything was exactly the same. I went to my mommy and showed her, and she kind of jumped all weird. She was all like, "You lost a tooth? I didn't know. When did that happen?"

"Yesterday. So I did everything for the Tooth Fairy on my own because I'm nine now and didn't want to bother you, but the Tooth Fairy didn't come."

Mommy told me that the Tooth Fairy isn't human, but she isn't perfect, either, and sometimes she forgets. "Maybe the Tooth Fairy will come tonight. She'll certainly visit you by the end of the week."

I mostly believe my mommy, but if the Tooth Fairy didn't come last night, she might never come back to my house again. Maybe she retired, and Mommy just doesn't know.

Mommy's been kind of distracted lately. After the whole thing with the counselor-who-wears-too-much-lipstick asking me if I was getting medicated, she and Daddy have been talking a whole lot when they think I'm asleep.

Daddy will say things like, "It really doesn't matter one way or the other, Karen. Just do whatever the school wants her to do."

Mommy will say, "But that's the whole problem! The school is trying to make it out like she's… like she's just some problem, or some statistic, and they can just solve it, no problem, with some pills. But she's fine, Cameron, she's… There's nothing wrong with her. I mean, it's probably genetic. Wasn't your dad kind of energetic too?"

Then, and this always happens whenever someone brings up Grandpa Claude, who died when Daddy was a teenager, Daddy will say, "Don't talk about my father."

And then Mommy will say, "Right. Sorry," but she says it in a way that sounds kind of mean. It sounds like she's making fun of him. Whenever Mommy sounds mean like that, I often have this weird empty sort of feeling right by my heart. It makes my chest hurt.

I think Mommy didn't even realize I'd lost a tooth because she's been so distracted. Good thing she's not the Tooth Fairy.

Now on to my second tragedy. I asked Mommy when the baby was coming (it's already been two months) and Mommy told me it's hopefully coming in another seven months.

Last time Mommy was pregnant, she got really sick. I am scared she'll get sick again and bleed over the tile on the kitchen floor. I'm not sure what my parents were thinking in making the baby take this long.

I said, "You could just have a baby faster."

Mommy looked at me like she was confused. "All babies take nine months to grow."

"Nuh-uh," I said. "Elizabeth Bayer got a baby brother from overseas in just two months, and her mommy never got pregnant at all."

"Yes," Mommy said, pinching her nose between two fingers like she always does when she has a headache coming on. "But Melanie Bayer adopted James. She didn't give birth to him."

"Yes. That's what you should do. Adopt a baby! That way it won't take too long."

Mommy sighed. "You need to learn how to have patience."

That's probably true, and it's something I'm working on with Dr. Keaty. I didn't know how to tell Mommy that I was really just scared we're going to lose a baby again.

A little bit frightened,

Miss W (with an extra tooth not in her mouth)

Dear the Man Upstairs,

I splashed in all the puddles I could during recess, and Mrs. N got mad and made me take off my shoes so I wouldn't drip mud all over the carpet, so then I had to complete Thursday's reading time with just socks on my feet. This was kind of sad because I was wearing my ladybug rain boots, which make my red hair look super nice and not out of place even though I'm the only person in the whole fourth grade with red hair. In fact, I'm also the only girl in the whole fourth grade with green eyes. But when I took off my boots, I realized that my socks weren't matching socks. Little Yvette Guiteau, the shortest girl in our class who wears two blond braids every day, remember? She sits in my table group, and she said, "Why on earth would you wear your socks like *that*?"

I kind of looked down at my feet. One was red and white striped and the other one had green and purple stars. I wiggled my toes. I mumbled, "I don't know."

Yvette gave me this nasty smile. "That's right. You don't know. It's because you don't know any better. That's what my mom says about you."

That was the kind of thing that made me feel like my heart was being squeezed all the way into a tiny box and it would never come out. I remember how Daddy said time flies when you're having fun, and I had a book about behaviors of queen bees in front of me, and bees are *always* fun, so I said really quietly, "It's reading time now, Yvette," and tried to read my book instead of thinking about adult mommies saying things about me behind my back, which, according to Grandma Jen, is one of the worst things you can do to someone. She often says, "Gossip by day, gossip by day, and burn forever the easy way." I tell her not to say the h-word because it's bad to curse, but the point is that gossip is bad, and Yvette's mommy needs to learn that because otherwise people's feelings will be hurt.

Before we were sent home, Mrs. N had an announcement. Our school has this thing called international week, where every class (and there are two classes in every grade) represents a country for a whole week. This year, like every year, Mrs. N's fourth grade class is going to be representing France. (Yvette was really excited because her grandma was born in France.) Mrs. N said that tomorrow the French teacher from the middle school, Mr. Dossier, is coming to our class to teach us how to speak French. Mrs. Young's class (the other fourth-grade class) is going to be Canada, like always. Momo is one of my other best friends (besides Nina), and she's in Mrs. Young's class, which is the only reason I care about the other class at all.

The cool thing is that when you get to fifth grade, the whole grade is America, and every kid gets a state. Except this year, I heard the teachers talking, and there are more than fifty kids in fifth grade, so someone is going to be Puerto Rico, and another person is going to be Guam.

In order to prepare for international week, my class will be performing a French song and bringing in baked goods. Mrs. N kept me after class with Nina and Jenna and said she wanted the three of us to present a ballet performance during the week. I'm really nervous because I've never danced in front of anyone before, and I don't want anyone to see me mess up and say, "Well, she didn't know any better." So, I guess, wish me luck!

Sincerely,

Miss W

PS

If it's raining because you're sad, I hope you feel better soon. Being sad is the opposite of fun.

Dear Miss W,

Pregnancies are scary. New life always is. It has been rain-ing recently because spring has come, and it is time for life to bloom anew. In previous letters, you've mentioned that you were worried the rain meant I was sad. I want to assure you that I send rain not as tears but as hope for flowers that will one day grow into things of beauty. Life is better when there are roses for you to stop and smell. Life is better when there is hope for new births. I am praying for your new sibling to grow strong and healthy. Sometimes, I need to remind myself to look for the things that bring me joy instead of focusing on all the things I find ugly. Like bullies.

Little Yvette Guiteau could stand to be a bit less concerned with other people and focus more on herself. The things she says about you are absolutely not true. There's nothing about you that you do because "you don't know any better." You, like the baby sister on the way and the flowers that I'm trying to help bloom, are growing. That's all you're supposed to be doing at this stage of life.

And, Miss W, I want you to know that it really is okay to be sad sometimes. Not everything has to be "okay because…" Time may pass faster when you're having fun, but it hurts people to hide all their feelings and pretend they don't exist. Reach out to someone you trust, maybe your doctor or mother or father when things go wrong. You are not alone.

Fondly,
the Man Upstairs

Dear the Man Upstairs,

Life *is* better when there are roses you can smell. Like this one time, Mommy and Daddy made me go on a hike I didn't want to go on. I was dragging my feet and pouting and doing the whole temper-tantrum thing. But then, as we were hiking by this lake near our house on a dirt path, there were these wildflowers that were yellow and pink. I actually don't remember what they smelled like, but I'm sure it was good because they made the hike much better. I want to say thank you because you make the sky rain, and the rain makes flowers. I'll eat flower nectar when I'm a bee.

Speaking of being a bee, because I'm in dance classes now, I have a special part in international week. Practice has been hard because it's during lunch hour. I keep getting fidgety during afternoon class because I haven't had enough time to run around with Nina and Momo (my best friend in the other class). A lot of what we do during practice is stand around and wait for Mrs. N to think about where she wants us. Standing around doing nothing is not my happy place. I also don't always have enough time to eat lunch. The other day in my afternoon music class with Mr. Heiki, I started munching on carrots and peanut butter.

Mr. Heiki said, "Miss W, there's no eating in this classroom."

I was close to starving from how hungry I felt. "Mr. Heiki, I'm really hungry. Can I please just finish this snack?"

Yvette leaned over to talk to one of Stupid Sean Hanner's friends, Pierce Morgan. "Why does she have to be such a baby all the time?"

I don't know if Pierce said anything back because for a second it felt like I couldn't hear anything at all, and then my cheeks felt like they were on fire, and I realized I was blushing a lot. It's not my fault I'm hungry, right? Anyone would be hungry if they didn't get to eat lunch.

Nina was sitting next to me, and she said, "Mr. Heiki, Miss W and I didn't get to eat lunch today because we were practicing for international week."

Mr. Heiki looked at me really hard for a second. "I'm sorry, but the rules are the rules. Put away your snack."

Yvette laughed again, and it felt like the whole class was looking at me packing away my little Tupperware of carrots and peanut butter. I tried to smile and be okay with everything, but it didn't work. I could feel my mouth shaking, and I realized that I was starting to cry. I did it really quietly, but I think a couple of people noticed. That made me wish I could dig a hole in the music room's carpet and jump inside and never come out.

I haven't even gotten any stickers this week because I haven't been able to sit still. On Friday morning, I forgot to take off my outside boots and sloshed water all over the wooden cubbies at the back of the classroom. Mrs. N got angry. And then in the afternoon class, I couldn't concentrate AT ALL, so I walked to the sliding cabinet doors (you know the kind of cabinet that looks like a wall but isn't?) and slid it open. I got out the toothpicks we keep there for projects and stuff and walked back to my desk with all the toothpicks.

Then when Mrs. N was teaching us about run-on sentences, I started trying to build a castle out of the toothpicks. I pulled out my container of Elmer's glue from my desk and started attaching the toothpicks to one another. I didn't even notice that some of the glue was drip-drip-dripping onto the desk. Instead, I started making triangles of toothpicks and putting them together to make a kind of large rectangle that would be the base of my castle. I'd made my first wall when I felt this presence behind me.

I turned around and Mrs. N was standing there, looking like Grandma Jen does when Mommy says something she really dislikes.

"What are you doing?" Mrs. N asked me quietly.

"Um," I said. "Making a castle?"

"And why," Mrs. N said, "are you making a castle right now?"

I didn't really have an answer, and I was starting to feel like maybe the fun of making a toothpick castle was not worth the feeling of embarrassment.

"Are those your toothpicks?" Mrs. N asked me.

"No," I said.

I think that maybe Mrs. N wanted to send me to the office because she looked really upset, but she took this great big breath and said, "You know the rules of this classroom: if you break it, you fix it."

I had to stay for twenty extra minutes after class to clean the glue off the desk, and then Mommy yelled at me in the car for wasting her time, and then Teacher Lara in ballet class wouldn't let me join the girls at the barre because I was late to her class, and then I had to watch ballet while I was stretching on the floor.

I got really worried about that, too, because I'm dancing for international week with Jenna and Nina. Both of them have been doing ballet since they were four, and I've only been doing it for about four months. I can't miss any more dance because then I'll never be good enough for the presentation, and I'll fall on my face and embarrass myself. Yvette Guiteau will laugh and laugh, and she'll never stop laughing at me.

Even though Mrs. N was mad at me on Friday, she told me after I cleaned the desk that, "I'm not mad at you. I believe in you, Miss W. I really do." That was kind of nice and kind of confusing because I'm not sure what Mrs. N believes I can do, but I still felt bad because Dr. Keaty always takes a moment during our lessons to reflect on the week. I realized that I'd been distracting a lot this last week. I thought I was making progress because Mommy told me so, but I guess not.

I don't think it matters in the long run, though. Bees don't have doctors or attention problems. That's why I'll be a great bee.

At any rate, this last Sunday was a terrible ending to a terrible week. It was our semi-annual (that means twice a year, I just learned) picnic with the Hanners. I get that Daddy and Mr. Hanner were like friends in college or something, but I hate the picnic both times a year. We always go out to Pike's Creek, and then we go to the grass and the adults get to sit on folding chairs and Stupid Sean Hanner, his little brother Pico Hanner, and I have to sit on scratchy blankets. This picnic, the Hanners were in charge of bringing the food, and all they had were deli sandwiches, which I didn't even want because I am going to be a bee. Bees do not eat meat. They eat flowers. I can't eat only flowers, though. I tried that for just one day, but then Mommy made me tell Dr. Keaty, and Dr. Keaty said that flowers don't have enough nutritional value to help growing girls like me be big and strong. We decided on a compromise: I can be a vegetarian.

Because I'm a vegetarian now, I told Mommy I would not eat the deli meat, and she said, "Don't be rude to your father's friend, dear."

I said, "It's really nice that you brought the food, Mr. Hanner, but no thank you."

Daddy said, "I'm so sorry about her, Dave. Kids, you know?" It felt like he was embarrassed, which I thought was unfair, because if anyone should have felt embarrassed, it was me, and I didn't.

Mr. Hanner laughed, Mrs. Hanner stared at me, and Stupid Sean Hanner took a big bite of his sandwich like he didn't care at all about me.

I decided to eat the bread only and ignore Stupid Sean Hanner for the rest of his stupid life. Fortunately, Grandma Jen had thought ahead, and she pulled out some crunchy peanut butter and jelly from her super cool yellow purse. I've decided that yellow is a cool color because bees are black and yellow.

But after lunch, the adults decided to play bridge, which is a four-person card game. Grandma Jen sat behind Mommy and told her whenever she thought Mommy was making the wrong play. This made Mommy upset, but that's not new because Grandma Jen and Mommy are always making each other upset. Stupid Sean Hanner and I went down by the creek.

Stupid Sean Hanner said, "Your hair is tied up today."

I had a cherry-print scrunchy holding up a ponytail, so I said, "It is."

He walked over to me and pulled the scrunchy out of my hair and tossed it into the creek. "Now your hair isn't tied up."

I had to wade into the creek to pick up the scrunchy, and it was too wet for me to use. Also, my shoes got soaked. I glared at him. "You're gonna pay for that."

He shrugged. "What are you going to do?"

I looked around and saw a caterpillar by the creek on the ground, and I reached down and picked it up and brought it close to his nose, and he said, "Get it away, get it away, get it away!" I felt bad, so I put the little critter back near the water.

He shuddered. "We should walk back to our parents."

I said, "Yes." So that's what we did.

We didn't talk to each other for the rest of the afternoon, which was fine by me because I think I wanted to say mean things to him. I know that it's not good to say mean things to people, even if they are stupid and throw your scrunchies into creeks.

When all of lunch was over, Grandma Jen drove me home, and we just talked for a while about the world and the many glories of bees. When we got to the apartment, Grandma Jen asked me to help her get towels to clean up the car because, "Why didn't you tell me that your shoes were wet?" And then we talked a little bit about my meetings with Dr. Keaty because Grandma Jen likes to stay up-to-date on my life even if she hates knowing anything about Mommy's life.

Sincerely,

Miss W

Dear the Man Upstairs,

It's been a whole day since the picnic with the Hanners, which means it's the first Monday of spring. Today, Stupid Sean decided to stay inside during lunch to watch Nina, Jenna, and I practice the dance for international week. I almost thought about telling Mrs. N that he should not be allowed in the classroom because he's a boy and I'm a girl. Anybody who's anybody knows that fourth grade girls and fourth grade boys should not be around each other unless absolutely necessary. In fact, I was going to tell her that, but then she said, "It'll be good practice for the three of you to get a sense of what it will feel like when you perform in front of an audience. Having Sean here to watch you guys will make you less nervous next week when you dance in front of your families."

I thought this was a bad reason to have Stupid Sean watching us because bees don't get nervous every time they do a dance. They're too busy to be nervous. They go from one place to the next, always working, and that's why I'll be a great bee. I'm never still for very long.

Some people say it's a problem that I move so much, and that's why I have Dr. Keaty. It's also why I have my chart for not moving during class, but I've been pretty bad at sitting still and not being disruptive for the past couple days. Mrs. N hasn't given me a sticker for the day for two weeks, but she hasn't yelled at me since Friday. Today she just gave me these big gray eyes that silently screamed, "I'm disappointed and think you could have done better."

But the thing is, I don't know if I can do better, but that's why I go to Dr. Keaty, you know, to learn how to do better. Sometimes I wish I didn't need Dr. Keaty, because Nina and Momo don't need to go to the doctor twice a week to learn "strategies" and I want to be normal too. But once I'm a bee, it won't matter because then the fact that I flit around everywhere and do everything won't be a problem at all because that's how bees are *supposed* to act, and I know that I'll fit right in to the hive. Bees don't make fun of each other, either; they all have their own job to do and they do it, and Yvette won't say things about me anymore once I'm a bee.

Except, even though bees don't get nervous, I guess I have a lot of room to grow, because I *was* nervous when Stupid Sean Hanner watched us. I even stumbled during one of my turns, which should not have been noticeable. But then it was noticeable because Jenna fell out of her spin. She tripped and fell sideways onto Nina, and then Nina lost her balance and dropped down to her knees, and then I stumbled because Jenna was where I needed to put my foot down after my little stumble, and I fell down, and then I landed next to Nina on the blue carpeted floor. Stupid Sean Hanner looked at Mrs.

N, blinked once, and said, "I think they might need some more practice, Mrs. N. Are they okay?"

So I launched myself to my feet, grabbed Nina and Jenna's hands, and dragged them to their feet. I crossed my arms and said, "We're fine. This was a…team-building exercise."

Nina giggled. "More like a team-falling exercise."

Jenna flushed bright red. "I'm so, so, sorry, guys. I just got kinda nervous, you know?"

And I wanted to say I didn't know because I want to be the kind of person who doesn't get nervous, but I do know, so me and Nina both nodded. Mrs. N said we were going to run the routine again, and Stupid Sean Hanner started eating his lunch *while* we were practicing. And I wasn't eating anything because I was practicing, but that doesn't mean I wasn't hungry.

And now I'm really nervous that we're all going to fall during the big performance, which would be really sad, but I'm also still hungry because Stupid Sean Hanner had like three iced cookies with his lunch, and he didn't offer to share even one, which is really quite rude if you ask me. Dancing is hard work, and I love cookies.

Mrs. N must be worried, too, because she didn't let us rest once during lunch and had us run our dance over and over again. Jenna said her feet hurt by the end. But because of all the dance practice, I was able to sit still during the whole afternoon. I was still disruptive this morning before dance practice. (I ended up trying to bounce my stress ball on the desk during math time because I was all finished with math and bored out of my mind, but it wasn't enough, so then I stood up and started throwing the ball from hand to hand and underneath one leg to the crook of my neck, but Mrs. N said, loudly, "That's enough. You know that's not what we're supposed to be doing right now.") But I was cool as a cucumber during history and reading time. After school got out, Mrs. N called me over and said she noticed that I was much more calm after I'd gotten energy out.

Mrs. N asked, "Have you thought about a career that's active? You seem to do well when you can move around a lot, and there are a lot of jobs that allow you to do that."

"I'm only nine and four-fifths, so I don't know a whole lot about jobs." Then I thought about it for a moment and realized, "I am trying to become a bee. And they're very active."

Mrs. N laughed at that like she thought it was adorable and funny. Bees are not something to laugh at; they are going extinct, and we need to save them.

Grandma Jen picked me up from school because Mommy had to go to a doctor's appointment because of the baby that's coming. Grandma Jen said, "That's one excuse I'll let your mother have."

"Excuse for what?" I asked.

"Never you mind," she answered. Then she told me she's going to come be a volunteer for international week and help the teachers set up tables, so I'll be able to spend all day with her next Tuesday. Daddy even agreed to take his lunch hour a little late so he can come see me dance. Daddy never takes off time from work, but he's doing it. Everyone's going to be there! (That makes me really scared I'll fall again, but hopefully, I'll be okay.) Can you come too? I'd love to see you face to face. Just knowing you'll be there will make me a lot less nervous.

Sincerely,

Miss W, the Ballerina and Bee-to-Be

Dear Miss W,

Sadly, I will not be able to attend your international week performance in person. I will instead be going on a vacation to the Himalayas. I try to be everywhere at once, and I need to take a little breather sometimes. I had already planned for a day off before I learned of your performance. I am afraid that I will have to miss it. I do hope that it goes well. I'm sure you'll do great. You always do. There's no reason to be nervous even if I won't be there. I have faith in you.

Are you still trying to act like a bee? I know you've been eating more than flowers, but I am curious about that. It seems like the picnic with the Hanners was a bit hard for you. I know that you would like to one day be an actual bee, but at the moment, you are still a human girl, and it might be good to honor that. Little girls like you can read, which bees can't do. They can send letters and write, which bees also can't do. Little girls can do so many things, so you should enjoy being one if you can. I think you are great as a girl.

Please tell me how this next week goes. I always enjoy our letters.

Best of Luck with your performance,
the Man Upstairs

Dear the Man Upstairs,

I've never, ever, heard about someone going to the Himalayas. I know all about the Himalayan mountains because, last year, I learned about continents and geography with Ms. Young. It's dangerous to climb to the top of the Himalayas because the air gets too thin to breathe. Are you visiting someone up there? Be careful!

I actually asked Grandma Jen if people can vacation there because she knows everything (even if Mommy likes to pretend she doesn't know anything) and Grandma Jen said, "That's not the weirdest thing I've ever heard."

I think you should go on your trip later. Daddy's taking a lunch break to come see me. He hasn't taken even one break from work in the last seven years. He doesn't even take sick days. If Daddy can do something so big for me, maybe you can go on your trip after international week, please? Dr. Keaty tells me that sometimes things in life don't go exactly the way we want them to, and that's okay too. Mommy says I'm going to need to start being more flexible once the baby comes. Maybe it's okay that you're not going to come. You still care about me, don't you? And I'll probably be really happy either way because it's so cool that Daddy is coming to watch me dance. And stressful. What if I make a mistake?

AND, even though I care about you, if we're going to stay friends, you CANNOT call me *little*. I am nine and four-fifths, and I know the square root of one hundred sixty-nine. Little girls don't know that, do they? And even if most bees can't read or write, I can. When I become a bee, I'll be the first insect who can read. I'll teach the other bees how to read and then there will be books for bees made out of flower petals. It will be wonderful, and we can still send each other letters.

But actually, I have been trying to act more like a girl. Dr. Keaty says I have to. Well, she doesn't say I have to, but she suggests it might be "worth considering the good parts of being a girl." She had me think of a list of things I like about being a girl after telling me it was okay if I didn't feel like a girl.

I told her I do feel like a girl. "I like wearing skirts and having scrunchies in my hair and playing pretend with Nina and Momo."

I then explained that Momo and Nina will still be my friends once I'm a bee and that girl bees have all the power in the hive. Dr. Keaty was wearing a fancy watch and when she leaned forward, her watch reflected the window's sunlight and made a rainbow on the wall. "Miss W," (she called me by my real name, but I don't think I can tell you until we've met each other in real life) and then she sighed. "Sometimes the world doesn't work the way we want it to. Bees are wonderful creatures, but at the moment, you are very much human. So are your mother and your grandmother and your best friends. Do you think you can learn to be proud of being a girl like them?"

Because of this, I stopped telling Mommy that I won't clean up my room because bees don't have rooms to clean. I don't want to worry anyone, and I can go back to being a bee when I'm older. I'm still taking dance classes. And Dr. Keaty is making me keep a journal about all the things I like about being a human girl. A big one right now is that human girls get to eat ice cream with their grandmothers and push their best friends on the swing sets.

I was done thinking about bees until Amy, my babysitter (and another human girl who's a good person), came over. She stayed with me Friday night. She had this biology textbook, and she read me a chapter she had on the behavior of bees. It even had diagrams! I love Amy.

She made me mac and cheese for dinner like she usually does, which is always amazing, and this time, she made it with flower-shaped pasta. She put an arm around my shoulders and said, "Bees eat flowers, don't they?"

It was super sweet, and it made me happy. Then I realized that I needed to tell her that even though the pasta was shaped like a flower, it wasn't actually a flower. No bee would eat it. I was like, "They do. Well, they actually eat the pollen, but that's from a flower. They don't eat pasta."

She was quiet for a second and then put on this bright smile. "But you eat pasta, don't you?"

I shook my head. "I don't eat pasta. Not when I'm trying to be a bee." If she'd just made me pasta that was shaped like pasta, I would have eaten it. But this pasta was sneaky and pretending to be something it wasn't, and that bothered me.

"Why don't you try to be a girl right now?" she asked me. "Girls can eat pasta that's shaped like flowers, can't they?"

I looked down at the mac and cheese, but I didn't want it anymore. It's one of my favorite foods most of the time, but it just reminded me that I wasn't a bee, and that made me kind of upset. "I don't want it."

Amy kept trying to get me to eat, but I kept saying no. She kept asking me *and* asking me *and moving* the bowl of pasta toward me, and I couldn't take it! I just wanted her to stop.

I got up from the table and pushed my bowl onto the floor, and it shattered. I stood near the broken ceramic, and I yelled, "I said no! I won't eat it! I won't, I won't, I won't!" A little bit of mac and cheese ran down my leg, and it felt kind of slimy.

Amy got red in the face and yelled right back at me, "Miss W! You *CANNOT* talk to me that way!"

Amy's never yelled at me before, never ever. I hated that I'd made her yell at me. Everyone yells at me. Mommy and Daddy and Mrs. N and even Grandma Jen sometimes. My lower lip started trembling and then I took a step back from Amy. My heel came down on a piece of ceramic, and it really hurt.

"Ow, ow, ow!" I looked at my heel and saw that I was bleeding just a little tiny bit. I can't be injured. I have a dance performance tomorrow! I need to be doing my best. Otherwise, I might fall!

Amy must have seen that I was bleeding, too, because she stopped looking so angry. "Don't move. Stay right there, and I'm gonna go get some shoes for me to put on and then we'll clean all this up."

I quietly said, "Okay."

She put on her shoes that she'd left at the front door. Then she walked over the broken bowl and picked me up and put me on the couch in the living room. She rubbed bacitracin over the small cut and put a Band-Aid on my foot.

She didn't say anything while she swept up the pottery in the kitchen and helped me get ready for bed without saying anything other than, "Brush your teeth. Wash your face. Change into your pajamas."

It took me a long time to fall asleep. It took so long Mommy and Daddy came home, and I heard them talking in hushed tones to Amy.

Mommy came into my room and whispered, "Miss W, are you awake?"

I said, "Yes, Mommy."

She walked over to my bed and put a hand on what she thought was my head, but was really my stuffed bear, Mr. Wiggles. "You can't yell at a babysitter or throw bowls on the floor. It's inappropriate. I'm disappointed with how you behaved tonight."

I didn't tell her that I was disappointed too. I just said, "Sorry, Mommy."

"I know you are." She didn't leave the room. Instead, she moved her hand around in the dark until she found my head. "Are you okay? I heard you got hurt."

I nodded into my pillow. "I'm okay, Mommy."

"That's good. Good." She started playing with my hair. She stayed until I fell asleep.

In the morning, Mommy acted like normal even though I felt like there was a pit in my stomach. Daddy wasn't around but that's okay because I'll see him for my performance later today. Amy will come see me again next week because Mommy's getting an ultrasound. I'm worried she hates me now.

There are only a few months before she leaves to go to college. She's going to the University of Michigan. What if I ruined everything last night?

Sincerely,

Miss W, a Girl Amy Babysits and Hopefully Doesn't Hate Too Much

PS

Did you ever go to college? Did going to college change you? I like Amy just the way she is. Wish me luck for later today! I'm worried.

Dear the Man Upstairs,

I didn't want to go to school this morning. I felt so bad about having made Amy get mad at me yesterday, and I had a cut on my foot.

Mommy said to me, "Get your backpack so I can drive you to school."

I flopped on the couch in our living room. "I can't go to school. I'm sick." I coughed twice to emphasize my point.

Mommy said, "You are not sick."

"What if the cut on my foot makes it impossible for me to dance? What then? I'll *die*."

Mommy opened the door to my room, and I couldn't see what she was doing in there because I was still on the couch, but several bangs later she came out holding my green and white striped backpack triumphantly. "If you die, then you die. It'll be character building. Now come on. I don't want to spend my morning like this over a cut the size of an atom."

"Atoms are too small to be seen, Mommy," I told her.

"Exactly," she agreed. "*Now*, Miss W, or we'll have a real problem. Get your stuff together. Last warning."

I did grab my backpack and follow Mommy into the elevator and out to the car even though I was freaking out the whole time. I could just see the future in front of my eyes. I was going to stumble on a turn and trip and bring Jenna and Nina down with me. Then Yvette would laugh at me and Daddy would say, "I left work for *this?*" And never talk to me ever again.

When I got to school, Grandma Jen waved hello at me from the field where she was setting up tables for international week with all the other volunteers. I waved hello back, then decided I was more of a hugger than a waver and ran to give her a hug.

"What's this for, then?" she asked me.

"Just love you," I mumbled into her shirt.

"It's mutual, my dear. I love you too. Now shoo! Go and learn something."

I gave her one last squeeze before I went up to my classroom. I still felt like there was something wrong with my stomach, but it was better than it had been.

Mrs. N spent the morning practicing our performance with us and getting us into top shape. At snack time, we were all allowed to go out to the international week fair, and it was a blast! I was having a good time running around with Nina and Momo, eating all the tacos I could because Mr. Laurence's third grade class was Mexico. We were all outside on the field, and the volunteers had set up cool tents by all the tables. I ignored Stupid Sean Hanner and his friends Pierce and Nathan, who were at the same table with us.

Momo stared dreamily into her taco. "Do you think I could serve tacos at my wedding?"

Nina rolled her eyes. "You're too young to get married."

Momo shook her head. "Am not. Well, maybe I am. But what about when I'm old enough? Can I serve tacos then?"

I took a bite of my taco and, mouth still of food but Mommy wasn't around to tell me to finish chewing, said, "If you got tacos like these, I'd come for sure. I think it's a great plan."

Stupid Sean Hanner and his friends Pierce and Nathan were listening, and Stupid Sean Hanner said, "Hey, if you like tacos that much, why don't you marry one?"

I don't know if he was talking to me or Momo but because he tends to be the kind of boy who teases me, I responded, "Because I don't think it's a good idea to eat your husband or wife. I'm pretty sure that's a crime, actually."

I don't know what Stupid Sean would have responded because at that moment, Mrs. N herded us like sheep back to the classroom, and he's six people behind me in line order.

When we got back to the classroom, Mrs. N gave us all this very stern kind of look. "Alright, dream team. This is the moment we've been working toward for a whole month. We're going to go out there and sing French like we were born in Paris and make our families proud."

I started sweating out of my palms because I knew that I was about to get on stage with just two other people after the song was over. We'd never had a perfect practice, but I'm also really good at getting distracted so I distracted myself by thinking about the sad excuse of juice Nathan brought.

He'd said that it was grape juice, but it was brown instead of purple and in a carton that had the label taken off. Mrs. N had put it on the top of the cubbies in our classroom instead of letting it go outside on the fourth-grade French table. It was gross. I named it Mr. Juice because clearly no one would ever drink it, and things we don't eat or drink deserve names.

We walked out of our classroom in line order. When we got out of the building, I saw Daddy and Mommy and Grandma Jen in the crowd, but I wasn't really looking at them. Our class got onto the stage that had been set up and sang our song. I don't remember that part at all. I was running the dance in my head and thinking about all the ways everything could go wrong.

When the song was over, everyone but Jenna and Nina and me left the stage. I remember looking out at all these faces as our music came on and thinking, *I can't do this.*

I felt a little bit like I was outside of my body during the first half of the dance. I could tell that I was dancing with the music and turning on the right counts, but I don't remember feeling like I was in control of what was happening. There's this part of the music where a flute lets out this high note. When that happened, it felt like I was suddenly back in my body. I kept moving and jumping and for the first time…I felt focused.

I felt free.

When the dance was over, Nina and Jenna and I all curtsied, and the crowd was clapping so hard I couldn't hear myself breathing. Everyone was on their feet. I wanted to do it all again.

Mrs. N was smiling at me like she does when someone does something right, and I never get that smile. At the end of the performance, I ran over to my family, and they were all so happy. Grandma Jen was grinning ear to ear. Mommy looked like she was fighting back tears.

Daddy gave me this one-sided smile, and his eyes looked at me like he was really *seeing* me, you know? "Good job up there, champ. You stole the show."

This meant a lot to me because Daddy often says, "Tough love is real love," so for him to tell me that I did well is a good sign.

(Though he also told me that Jenna bumped into Nina during the performance and that I should have just done a solo.)

Grandma Jen said, "You looked so beautiful up there, my love. Even better than a bee, if you ask me. Which you didn't, but I answered anyway. I couldn't be prouder."

Mommy lost her fight against the tears and couldn't even talk because she was crying so hard. She tried to say something that sounded like, "I knew you could do it," but it was all garbled. Apparently, sometimes people cry when they're happy.

Sincerely,

Miss W, the Principal Dancer

PS

This was the only day I can remember where I didn't feel a need to be "disruptive" or anything. I had something to do the whole day. It was really nice. I wish I could feel like that all the time.

PPS

How's your vacation in the Himalayas going?

Dear Miss W,

I have returned from my vacation. It was wonderful, thank you for asking. I enjoyed that it was calm and restful.

I am so glad international week went well for you. The dance you performed seems wonderful, and I am sorry to have missed it. You are right that sometimes people cry when they are happy. It can be confusing, but I am pleased both your parents were happy for you.

I wonder, with all the letters you have been sending to me, has your writing improved over the course of this year? I do think that you seem to be better at expressing yourself recently.

And to answer a previous question of yours, I do not recall if I went to college. If I went, I went to more than one place. But who can say, really? It was so long ago. The most important thing, my dear, is to remember that there is always more to learn.

Until next time,
the Man Upstairs

Dear the Man Upstairs,

That's a good question! I think I've been getting better at writing. Mrs. N has actually said that it keeps getting better and better, so I think these letters to you are helping. I probably write more often than anyone else in the fourth grade. Dr. Keaty tells me that it's really amazing I have the patience to sit and write to you. I am pretty amazing after all. I do sometimes have to get up and move around and then come back, but I always come back, and that's what Daddy says will make me a winner.

Speaking of being a winner, I thought that bees were winners, but I'm letting that go. Remember when Amy showed me about bees in her biology book?

This morning, I begged Mommy to take me to the library so I could read more about them. I got into this one book that had a whole chapter on bees. It was all like "the women are more important," and I was thinking, *Yep,* and then it was all like, "and there's a queen," and I was thinking, *That'll be me,* and then it was like "the bees do a dance to explain where to find food," and I was like *Check, I'm in dance.*

But then it said, "The average lifespan of a worker bee is three months, and the average life of the queen is four years."

I don't want to live for just four years. Actually, I'm almost ten. I'm too old already. I started crying, and I couldn't stop. Mommy couldn't understand why a science book made me cry so much. She took me outside to the library's parking lot, said something like, "What am I going to do with you?" and then got on her knees and hugged me until I stopped crying. She even got her nice pants dirty and only complained about that six times on the car ride home.

After I calmed down, I answered her question about what she should do with me. "You should keep doing what you've been doing with me, but maybe be a bit nicer to me sometimes? Sometimes the way you talk to me makes me feel like there's something wrong with me."

She tried to laugh but just looked like she was going to cry too. "There's *nothing* wrong with you. And I'm plenty nice."

I mumbled, "Most of the time," but she didn't hear me, and that's probably a good thing.

She asked me why I started crying, and I explained about the bees. She took one look at me and said, "Well, in that case, you'll just have to settle for being human." Daddy sometimes says he settled for living in an apartment. I didn't feel like I wanted to settle for being human, though. I just don't want to die really soon. I didn't really know what to feel. It just seemed like the whole sky was falling, and I was the only person who could tell.

Are you human? Did you have to settle to become the Man Upstairs? Either way, I've decided. I will go to Aspen High School. Because if I can't be a bee, I want to be a teenager. Maybe I'll become a teenager who studies bees, and I'll live with the bees as a human friend and then it won't matter that

I can't sit still. Both Amy, the babysitter, who I hope doesn't hate me and who I will see soon, and Grandma Jen went to Aspen High. Daddy went to some school in Colorado because that was where Grandpa Claude was working. I guess I could go there too.

I just want to wear makeup and sing in the cafeteria like that blonde girl on TV in the videos Mommy likes to watch when she thinks I'm asleep. I have red hair, so maybe I'll have to be one of the back-up dancers. That's perfect though. I'm in dance. And Mommy says I can't carry a tune. According to Daddy, I have three more years before I'm a teenager and four more years before I'll go to high school. But he also says, "Time flies when you're having fun," so I'm going to have as much fun as I can. Wish me luck in becoming a teenager! I can't wait to be one. Maybe by then I won't need Dr. Keaty anymore.

From,

Miss W, a Girl Who Is Not and Will Never Be a Bee

PART II

LARVA

Dear the Man Upstairs,

Remember how I was hoping I wouldn't need Dr. Keaty anymore when I was a teenager? I'm still hoping that. I'm only a fourth grader, and I need her right now. I wish I could just go to school and not have to worry about getting yelled at.

I got sent home, and it wasn't even my fault. See, Mrs. N went away to a teacher's conference she says she goes to every May. She had a substitute teacher come in. The substitute was named Mr. Yee, and he was all serious when he wrote his name on the whiteboard.

He said that even though he was a substitute, he wasn't going to just let us "goof off," and I thought that it would be a good thing. I always do my work best as I can. Only, Mrs. N and I have a system now. I can get up and walk around sometimes during class when people are doing individual work if I'm already done. She lets me go out into the hallway, and she'll call me back when individual work time is over. She and Dr. Keaty and Mommy had a conversation about it, and she decided this would work best because I don't distract anyone if I go walk in the hall *after* I've already finished my work.

Mr. Yee didn't know about the system. He assigned us long division worksheets, and I'm great at long division because numbers are just numbers. I finished the worksheet in like three minutes.

Daddy makes me do math worksheets whenever Mommy is busy. He works from home two days a week because he can spend that time talking to donors for the no-pay clinic he's a doctor at. He's hoping to one day spend all his time doing development, which means asking for money because he doesn't like being around his patients very much. He needs it to be capital *Q* Quiet when he is working. He gives me the math sheets because he says it's easier for him to help me with math every now and again than it is to spend time talking to me.

Sometimes I wish he was a better listener to me and wanted to hear me talk. Back when I was six, Daddy stopped listening to me. Mommy and Daddy were going to have a baby. Mommy's belly had a little bump, and we even knew the baby was going to be a boy. But then Mommy got sick. Sometimes, when babies stop growing, they can't be born. Grandma Jen says my baby brother went to heaven early because he was so beautiful. I cried about it for a whole week. Sometimes I still wonder about what he would have been like. I think that when my baby brother stopped growing, Daddy started wilting and forgot how to stand tall. I know I talk too much and too fast. Mommy always tells me to slow down. Daddy always says that if I could just be quiet, maybe he could *finally* do some work. He works a lot now and doesn't talk to me, and that's why we do so many math worksheets.

I practice math a lot, so I finished the worksheet in class early. I went out into the hallway to work off some energy because I felt like I was going to buzz out of my skin. That happens sometimes when I focus on something for too long. But Mr. Yee stuck his head out the door not a second later and yelled, "What do you think you are doing? I thought I made my expectations for this class perfectly clear."

I said, "Well, Mrs. N said—"

He had a mustache, and it bobbed up and down as he cut me off with, "Don't use that excuse on me. I'm sure Mrs. N did *not* give you permission to go running out of class and off to who knows where."

"But she did, I promise, she lets me do it all the time!" And I yelled that part a little loud, and then he got really mad at me, and then he said he was going to send me to the office for yelling at a teacher. He wrote me a note and then I went to the office. I stomped the whole way there because I was so angry at how unfair everything was.

This is the fifth time I was sent to the office this year, so then Mrs. Page (the secretary) told me she had to phone home. She needed to have them collect me and set up a meeting because that's the policy at Nelson Elementary: five office visits means there's a pattern that needs to be examined.

But Mommy was at a yoga class for pregnant women that she thinks will help her keep the baby this time and Daddy was working, so Grandma Jen came to pick me up. I got into her old Cadillac, and she drove me to Baskin-Robbins.

She took one look at me, and I was really upset but I kept on smiling because people say when you're happy time passes by faster, and maybe I'll grow up faster and then by the time I'm a teenager, I won't have to feel like this anymore. Grandma Jen said, "Ice cream is good for when you're celebrating and for when you're crying."

And I said, "I'm not crying."

"Not yet." And then she asked me what happened, and then I did start to cry.

Sincerely,

Miss W, A Girl Who Got Sent Home UNFAIRLY

Dear the Man Upstairs,

I cried the whole drive home and then got out of the car sniffling and walked up the seven floors to my apartment holding Grandma Jen's hand and hoping really desperately for a tissue.

When Grandma Jen and I got inside, she brought me to the bathroom. "Come on now, let's wash that face of yours."

And I was feeling a little bit cheeky because I can be with her, so I said, "Let's wash *your* face."

Grandma Jen patted my cheek and said, "You're awful cute, dear," and then wet a washcloth and rubbed it all over my face like I was a baby cat being groomed.

I said, "This feels not good, Grandma Jen," and she ignored me for two more minutes and then put the washcloth away.

She said, "Well, now it's over so it feels like nothing."

I said, "You can't feel nothing. There's nothing to feel when you feel nothing, so you don't feel it."

She guided me out of the bathroom and nodded. "That's an interesting philosophy I'm not sure makes sense. You know what would make sense? Cookies." And I agreed because cookies and I are best friends.

Mommy got home from yoga when Grandma Jen and I were frosting our new creations in the apartment, and she got really upset. "Jen, why on earth would you take my daughter out of school to make *cookies*? Of all things to do, honestly. She shouldn't even be eating much sugar. You know it will make her hyper."

And I was feeling a little hyper to be honest because I'd already had ice cream and then I'd had cookies, too, and also my tummy was hurting a little bit and I kind of felt like maybe I needed to run up the walls and throw up at the same time.

Grandma Jen said, "Well, dear, the school called you and then Cameron and then me, because she needed to come home. Something about office visit number five? You might try saying thank you that I was available so you could finish your ridiculous attempt at exercise."

Grandma Jen's never been very nice to Mommy, but Mommy's been trying so hard recently to keep the baby that she found a Facebook group to help her out. There's this essential oil specialist named Clover Mommy's been getting advice from, and Grandma Jen always tells Mommy that she's being stupid. Sometimes when they argue, I want to hide under my bed.

I sniffled a bit because when I cry, I go all out, and a washcloth can only do so much to help the general mess that was my face after a meltdown. "Don't worry, Mommy. I like cookies." I was hoping Mommy would say something like, "Oh, well that's fine then," and then she and Grandma Jen wouldn't fight at all.

Instead Mommy said, "But sometimes we don't get to have things we like and that's life." And then she paled and muttered, "Five visits? Oh, heck," but she said a bad word, by the way. I thought you should know.

She walked into our teeny-tiny kitchen and kneeled in front of me. "Baby, why were you sent to the office? Were you sick?" She put a hand to my forehead even as I was shaking my head.

But I did feel kind of queasy from all the ice cream and cookies, and I almost threw up for real. Mommy was looking at me like I really was sick, but that was wrong, so I said, "No, it wasn't my fault, but we had a substitute, and I went into the hall like I can do with Mrs. N, but he got mad at me and then he sent me to the office and then—"

But Mommy was looking through her phone because I know that parents get alerts for why their kids are sent home and then she said, quiet and intense, "You yelled at a teacher?"

And I said, small, "I didn't mean to, promise."

And she said, voice deep and dark, "Go to your room."

Then Grandma Jen said, "Karen, she's right, that sub was a piece of work."

But Mommy stood up and glared at Grandma Jen. "I am her mother, and I am telling her to go to her room. You can leave now, Jen."

I went off to my room, but we're in an apartment and the walls are pretty thin. Grandma Jen was saying, "It was a hard day for her, and I think you need to be there for her right now."

But then Mommy yelled, "And who is here for me right now, huh? Do you know what happens now? I need to go talk to Vice Principal Viceport for the third time this year and try to keep my daughter out of special ed. I only managed to keep her out last time because Dr. Keaty agreed to talk to Mrs. N with me. They keep saying that maybe she's just too hard to control in the classroom. They keep trying to *medicate* her. Even Dr. Keaty! And you're trying to say I need to parent my child better? She's not your daughter, and you're not the one living with her full time, so just stop, alright? Just stop."

Grandma Jen said something too low for me to hear and then Mommy said, "I think I told you to leave."

And then I stopped listening and went to my bed and sat down on my purple comforter and swung my legs and thought of all the things I wanted to say and all the things I wanted to yell and how I wished I'd never gone out into the hallway and annoyed Mr. Yee.

And then I went to my desk and pulled out some math worksheets because I felt like if I did anything else I might start crying again, but numbers are just numbers. Mr. Wiggles, my stuffed bear, reminded me that I had managed to hide no less than four cookies in my pockets, and those helped too, even if they made me feel even more sick than I already felt. I ate them under my bed.

Sincerely,

Miss W

PS

Do you have any advice for me?

Dear Miss W,

It sounds like things are a little bit tough right now, and I'm sorry. Has your Dad said anything about what's happening with the fifth office visit?

I know you probably feel like everything is hard and sad, but I promise it will get better. If life were full of only happiness, no one would ever grow. You want to become a teenager as fast as you can, but I think childhood is something to be treasured. Even so, this moment right now, when you are sad and learning to pick yourself up, this is what growing up feels like.

Growing up is filled with hard things, and wonderful things, and the moments you want to remember forever. There will be times when you will be so angry and times when you will be so joyful, and every day will help you become the woman you will one day be.

My advice to you is to remember all the things that are still good in your life. Remember your friends Momo and Nina, stick your tongue out at Sean Hanner, have fun in your dance class. There's no sadness that lasts forever, my dear.

Wishing you well,

The Man Upstairs

Dear the Man Upstairs,

Daddy definitely has thoughts about me and the "Five-Office-Visit Situation" (which I've also been calling "The Substitute Teacher Who Ruined my Life Situation"). After Mommy made Grandma Jen leave the apartment, Mommy didn't let me out of my room, which was terrible because I really needed to move around. But I couldn't, so I crawled out from under my bed and sat with Mr. Wiggles on my lap at my desk. I kept working on my math worksheets. I couldn't do that for too long because I'd had ice cream AND cookies so then I decided to jump up and down on my bed for a while. Mommy says I'm not allowed to jump on my bed, but Mommy is the person who made me stay in my room. I jumped and jumped and thought that maybe Mommy would come into my room to tell me to stop, but she didn't. I got tired and bored after a long time of jumping, so then I went back to my math worksheets.

Well, a few hours later, or at least what *felt* like a few hours later, Daddy came home while I was in my room practicing long division. Daddy said, and I could hear him really well because he always talks loudly when he gets home from work because he listens to rock music in his car, "Where's the champ?"

Mommy said, "She's in a time-out. She was sent home today for yelling at a teacher."

Daddy said, "Oh yeah, Mom phoned on the commute and told me all about that. Real piece of work, that sub was. Good for her."

And then Mommy yelled, "No! Not good for her! Now we have to go talk to the principal."

Daddy was not concerned. "Well, you have to do that. I've got work."

Mommy said, like she couldn't believe she had to say this, (like she says to me sometimes, "No, you can't practice your splits, we are at CHURCH."), "You have *work?*" She paused for a moment and then said, quiet enough I had to strain my ears against the door, "You have a *daughter.*"

Daddy didn't wait one moment before replying, sharply, "You think I don't know that? I have a daughter that I *work* to support. And a wife I work to support as well. And now a doctor I pay to help out the daughter. I am fully aware that I have one child, Karen."

And then they were arguing with each other, but I decided that I'd had enough of being in my room, and I left and walked out into the common room. Daddy and Mommy stopped talking and looked at me.

"Um," I said, "I haven't had any dinner tonight. Could I maybe eat with Nina's family?"

Mommy started saying, "I think I told you to be in your room and—" but Daddy cut her off and said, firmly, "That's a great idea. I'll call Yerena right now." Mommy gave Daddy a big glare with narrowed green eyes.

"Don't you think we should discuss this together?" she asked.

Daddy didn't say anything, just loosened the tie around his neck and held his smartphone up to his ear. "Hello, Yerena? Hi, it's me, Cameron. Oh, everything is fine! Mm hmm, mm hmm, yeah. Well, she was wondering if maybe she could get dinner with Nina? We're swamped here. Mm hmm. Oh, great, thanks. We owe you one."

He put the phone into his pocket. "Right, so Yerena will be here in ten minutes."

Mommy didn't say anything else to Daddy or me until Yerena came. Then she gave me one of her strict looks and said, "Be good."

I almost said, "I always try to be," but I felt like my mouth was too dry to say anything to her.

Nina was already in the car when I got there, and her light brown hair was still in a bun from dance class. We got to her house, and I went to her room and turned my back while she changed out of her leotard, talking to me about her teacher the whole time. "My ballet teacher is really strict, but he cares about us, you know?" I'll have him if I get moved up next year!

She and I were both happy to eat dinner together. Her mom made us lasagna because lasagna is a staple in Nina's house. Nina could tell I was a bit sad because she and I basically share a mind we're so close, but she decided the best thing to do was to braid my hair and tell me all about her newest crush, Christopher Diggle in the other class. I let her talk to me about him, even though I know from Susan Woodson that he picks his nose. Nina's cute when she has a crush, and she was so bubbly. I didn't tell her about Christopher's nose picking behavior.

But then Nina said that she didn't know what to get me for my birthday this week, and I nearly fell out of my chair. I almost forgot that my birthday was coming up! I'll be ten in just two days. Wish me luck.

Sincerely,

Miss W, a Girl Who Is Almost Ten

P.S.

Mommy and Daddy weren't talking to each other when I got home. I've never seen them like this before. Do you think they'll be okay?

Dear Miss W,

No relationship is perfect. Relationships are hard work. Very rarely do parents get along with one another all the time.

That does not mean that arguing will always lead to things going wrong. Sometimes we argue with the people we love because we love them. The opposite of love is not anger or hatred, it is not caring about someone at all.

Your parents seem to care about each other very much. I believe that they will fight sometimes and argue sometimes and come out all the stronger for it. Have faith.

Fondly,
the Man Upstairs

Dear the Man Upstairs,

I hope you're right. Mommy and Daddy are still arguing, which means that Mommy has stopped making breakfast for Daddy, and Daddy has stopped giving her back rubs, and both of them are ignoring me a little because they are so focused on being mad at each other and a little bit at the substitute teacher, Mr. Yee.

Mommy has to go talk to the principal tomorrow, but today is my birthday. An unexpected thing happened to me at school. I was playing zombies with Nina and Momo (we go to the kindergartners with our arms stretched out and scare them terribly, except teeny-tiny Marilyn Doover always runs up and hugs us, and we sometimes let her be a zombie, too) when Stupid Sean Hanner came over kicking up little rocks. He said, in the tone of voice Mommy says burns her ears, "Happy Birthday," rolled his eyes, and then gave me a bag of frosted cookies from behind his back.

At first, I thought they were poisoned, and I eyed him suspiciously.

"You eat one," I challenged, and then he did and seemed fine, so then I took the bag.

"Me too! Me too!" Nina cried, because she loves cookies and likes Stupid Sean Hanner better than I do, and so I gave her one.

Then I said, "Thanks!" and Sean Hanner did this weird thing where he stretched his lips, I think he was trying to smile, and went away to go play with Nathan without saying anything back. I thought he had been nice, but then I realized his evil plans. Nina and I were swarmed by hordes of kindergartners trying to get the cookies. I almost lost my hair ribbon.

Mommy, Daddy, Grandma Jen, and I all had a birthday dinner together after school, but it was really weird.

Grandma Jen asked me, "How was your day?"

And I said, "It was good."

Daddy said, "That's so wonderful. Isn't it, Mom?"

And Grandma Jen said, "It is wonderful, Cameron."

Mommy said, "Are you having a good birthday?"

So I said, "Yes, I am," because I was.

Then Mommy said, "That's good," but Grandma Jen and Daddy didn't say anything to her.

I spent the whole dinner having conversations with just Daddy and Grandma Jen or just Mommy because they wouldn't talk to each other at all.

Mommy and Daddy had to go to another doctor's appointment for the baby, so then Grandma Jen and I drove back to the apartment and just sat on our blue couch and talked for a while. I was happy to talk to Grandma Jen because Mommy and doctors make me scared about her losing the baby again. Grandma Jen distracted me and was surprised to learn that I didn't want to be a bee anymore. She was super proud of how I was handling everything in class.

She said, "I'm on your side."

It's nice to have people on your side.

Sincerely,

Miss W

PS

I'm pretty wise now, see? I'm a ten-year-old. I hope the meeting with the principal goes well, but I have a bad feeling. Do you?

Dear Miss W,

Happy belated birthday! I don't know if I can even remember my birthday, I've been around for such a long time. I feel like I celebrate my birthday with every new year because I grow with the world.

It sounds like Sean Hanner and Nina are good friends. As I'm sure you remember, your grandmother is my friend, and now, so are you. Having people on your side is incredibly important. There have been times in my life when I have seen people turn away from me and pursue other relationships, but many people will come back.

I cannot tell you how the meeting with the principal will go. No matter what happens, remember that you are a remarkable young woman.

Wishing you well,

the Man Upstairs

PS

Attached to this note is a Snickers bar to celebrate all your accomplishments. Congratulations on turning ten.

Dear the Man Upstairs,

Thank you so much for the Snickers bar! It was the perfect birthday gift. I feel like you and the Tooth Fairy must be friends because you both give me the same thing. Except, the Tooth Fairy gives me smaller bars, and only when I lose a tooth, not on my birthday, so maybe you two aren't so alike after all.

I don't know what happened today when Mommy had the meeting because I wasn't allowed to be a part of it. Ms. Page said that I was "too young," and that I should, "please go back to recess and stop asking me if you can be part of the conversation." I had this bubbling feeling under my skin, like I was itching on the inside, and I really wanted to know what was happening in the meeting. But Ms. Page shooed me away. So then I went to go play with Nina and Momo, and we made fairy houses in the school garden using twigs and branches. Stupid Sean Hanner stuck his tongue out at me from where he was swinging with Nathan, and I glared at him.

Momo said, "He likes you."

And I said, "He does not."

Nina shrugged. "Well, I like Gregory Vincent."

But I was all confused because that was new information. "I thought you liked Christopher Diggle."

Nina wrinkled her brow. "I did, but he picks his nose. Susan Woodson told me."

I don't know anything about Gregory Vincent except that he's a fifth grader in Mr. Odber's class. I think he's too old for Nina, and I told her, but then Momo said, "No one is too young for love. I would know because my mom's a family counselor. She says even babies love their parents."

I think something about her logic was wrong, but I was too antsy to think about it that hard. I could just see Mommy and the teachers deciding I couldn't be at school anymore because I was too distracting. I couldn't focus at all. That was okay because it's almost the end of the year, so we were just watching a movie in class. Mrs. N let me stretch on the floor.

I think she feels bad about Mr. Yee because she went out of her way to tell me that I am smart and stuff today. I thought that was weird because I didn't think she liked me very much.

Mommy was anxious on the car ride to Dr. Keaty's. I asked her how the meeting went, and she said, "Fine," which wasn't really an answer, but she looked kinda scary, like that video Nina showed me on her smartphone (I want one so bad) of the raccoon who got spooked and then attacked an old man's leg, and I like my legs, so I didn't ask any more questions.

Meetings with Dr. Keaty are always similar; she asks me about my week and then asks me more questions. I can talk as much as I like with her because that's the whole point. Except today Mommy came in with me to the appointment.

Dr. Keaty asked, "Did the conversation with the school go well?" And I didn't even know Dr. Keaty knew about the meeting.

Mommy was slumping on the couch. "Yeah, I mean, yes. But they have some main concerns that they want you to work on with her."

Dr. Keaty smiled a little. "I'd be happy to help. What do they want us to work on?"

Dr. Keaty always does that, makes it about "us," instead of "me," and I don't know why but I like it.

Mommy said, "Ms. Page and Vice Principal Viceport made this checklist for fifth grade readiness. Miss W needs to be able to check off everything on the list by the end of the summer or they might move her into," Mommy lowered her voice as if that meant I wouldn't be able to hear her, but I still could, "into the special needs program."

Dr. Keaty just nodded even though I could feel my breaths coming faster. "Please forward me that list."

Mommy said, "I will."

"Do you still have the same stance on medication?"

Mommy said, firmly, "I do."

I asked, "What medications?"

Mommy said, "None," and left it at that. I wondered if maybe Mommy was a little sick. Sick people need medication.

I got to look at the big list after Mommy went to the other room. It had seven headings: *Direction and Rules, Attention, Collaboration, Performance, Time Control, Behavior,* and *Emotion.* Each heading had several bullet points underneath it filled with things I need to do. It felt really overwhelming and the words began to swim. I don't want to go to the special needs program. I have more energy than Nina and Momo, but they're still my friends and I don't want to leave them. I'm not that different from other kids, am I? I felt like the room was spinning.

Dr. Keaty must have gotten out of her seat because the next thing I saw were her purple shoes. She laid a hand on my shoulder, and I looked into her deep brown eyes. She gave me a kind smile. "You're okay," she said. "We *will* get through this."

I nodded and felt myself relax a little bit. She squeezed my shoulder once before going back to her seat. "What do you want to work on the most today?"

Dr. Keaty does that a lot, too—gives me choices. We talked about my friends today because one point under collaboration is, "has positive social interactions with peers."

After the meeting, Mommy drove me home and told me, "It's time you start helping out a little more around the house. You're ten years old, and I am not your slave." I have new chores: I have to empty the dishwasher and sweep after dinner. I don't like doing either of those things.

Now that I have more things I need to do, sometimes I miss being nine. Except, I really want to be a teenager as soon as I can, and I guess this is just the first step. When I'm a teenager, I'll be old enough and strong enough that no one will ever yell at me. Maybe I won't need Dr. Keaty then, either. I asked Mommy if I would have less jobs when I become a high schooler and she laughed and said, "Oh, no, you only get more from here. Especially with your sibling on the way." I wish I would grow up already and that my baby sibling would get here already because I'm not very good at waiting or worrying that she'll join our baby brother in heaven.

Still a little bit worried,

Miss W

PS

Mommy seems even more mad at Daddy today. I think it's because he didn't ask her at all about the meeting.

Dear the Man Upstairs,

Mommy and Daddy are so mad at each other they've stopped talking to each other very often. Daddy started working from the Starbucks near our apartment on his days away from the clinic to avoid talking to Mommy. I kind of miss him, but not as much as I miss the Daddy from before I was six who used to take me mini-golfing and buy me soft pretzels. Summer is only a day away, and I really hope Mommy and Daddy won't be mad at each other all summer.

Mommy's joined another Facebook group for homeschooled children. The other night, Daddy was reading a book about something called Chernobyl while eating dinner so he wouldn't have to talk to Mommy or me. Mommy snapped her fingers in front of his face and said, "I'm learning how to homeschool from this group because I refuse to let our daughter join special ed. Nothing is *that* wrong with her."

That felt a little bit mean, and I wished that I had brought Mr. Wiggles with me to dinner. I really don't want Mommy to homeschool me because I don't think she'd be a patient teacher.

Daddy raised his eyes and mumbled something along the lines of, "Do whatever you want, Karen," before turning back to reading his book while eating his lasagna.

Mommy blinked a couple of times really fast and then rubbed a hand over her belly and whispered, "I bet you'll be interested in what I have to say when you come, won't you, baby?"

I almost answered her that I am almost always interested in what she has to say even if I don't always like it when I realized Mommy wasn't talking to me but the baby in her stomach. I've started calling my unborn sister "Anthophila" in my head because that's the scientific name for bee and even if I know I can't be one anymore, I still like them.

Then I blinked really fast a couple of times. No one ever talks to *me* anymore.

After dinner, Mommy and Daddy didn't really seem like they wanted to hang out with me, which was lonely. It was still light outside, so I went down the seven flights of stairs from our apartment. Our apartment has a grassy area by the pool. I'm allowed to go down to the pool as long as I leave a note with our refrigerator magnets saying, "gne dnstrs." (I think that's what texting will be like when I finally get a phone.) The sun was setting, and the air was sticky and wet and hot, so I was glad that I was wearing just an old tank top and shorts. I lay down with my head on the lawn and looked up at the sky. The clouds were painted red and yellow and orange, and I thought that maybe you were up there. That felt less lonely. Were you?

I didn't think about how scary it is that I might not be allowed to stay in school with my friends next year. I worry about that almost all of the time now. It was peaceful for a second in my mind.

When it was dark, I walked back up to my apartment. Mommy was sitting on the couch all leaning over her computer and kind of startled when she saw me.

"Oh, it's you. You scared me," she said.

"I'm not very scary," I replied and gave her my brightest smile. "See? Scary people don't smile like this."

Mommy relaxed back into the cushions. "I suppose they don't." She sighed. "You have grass in your hair."

I lifted a hand to my head and ran it through my red curls. Some grass found its way to my fingertips. "So I do."

"Go take a shower," she said.

When I washed the grass and dirt off and watched it going down the drain, it felt like *I* was the thing getting washed away. This dizzy and nauseous feeling hasn't gone away. I really hope that next year I can stay with all my friends.

From,

Miss W

Dear the Man Upstairs,

I woke up on the last day of school with wet hair from the shower I'd taken the night before and a feeling like maybe I needed to throw up. I didn't and put on a smile because I didn't want anyone asking me, "What's wrong?" (Or not asking. That might be worse.)

The last day of school was filled with yearbook signing and me trying to get every single person in our grade to sign mine because I don't know if I'll be coming back next year. Mommy says that it all depends on me and how good I'll be able to be. (It feels like a lot of pressure.) The only person who wouldn't sign my book was Yvette. She also didn't ask me to sign hers. Samantha, Yvette's best friend who is also mean, did sign mine.

Mrs. N saw me going around and trying to get everyone included in the book (I even went to the other class, but that was mostly because Momo is one of my best friends and she's in the other class) and she waved me over to her desk.

She put out her hands. "Can I sign your yearbook, too?"

I beamed big and wide because of course she can. She's *Mrs. N*, which means she's a teacher and therefore all-powerful in the classroom. "Yes! That'd be great, Mrs. N."

She gave me a smile in return, which was maybe the third time she's smiled at me all year, and then took up half a page writing me a message before she handed my book to me. Then she asked, "Would you sign mine, too?"

I didn't even know that teachers get yearbooks, but I nodded so hard I thought my ponytail might come out. She slid me her book, and I thought for a moment.

I ended up writing her a letter that talked about how amazing a teacher she is and thanking her for coming up with things for me to do when I have so much energy I feel like I'll explode. I ended it by saying, *Everyone always tells me to do my best, and I think you are one of the people in my life who allows me to be my best whenever I can be, so thank you.*

I left after hugging Nina and Momo extra tight in case I can't stay in school with them and even waved goodbye to Stupid Sean Hanner before going to get ice cream with Grandma Jen.

Summer began today. I was sitting at our tiny kitchen table, noticing that my legs were swinging less far above the floor than last year, when I heard the muffled and intense voices behind the door of my parents' room that only happen when they are talking about something very important. They didn't sound angry though, which I thought was a good sign. They haven't talked for so long in a while.

Because whatever they were talking about seemed very interesting, I did the only logical thing to do: I pressed my ear against their bedroom door to hear better.

Mommy was saying, "Oh, but I like the open feel of it."

Daddy said, "Yes, but I feel like privacy in this one might be an issue."

Then Mommy said, "What about the Tudor-style home, the one across town?"

Daddy said, "Yes, that one is good too."

Mommy said, "So, we've narrowed it down to three?"

Daddy said, "We have. We'll need Mom's opinion. She'll skin us alive if we don't listen to her wise judgment." I heard muffled laughter.

Then Mommy said, "So, let's go house-hunting today. We'll need our little bee's opinion too."

Daddy said, "She'll be happy anywhere with a yard big enough."

I heard footsteps approaching, so in my trained ninja fashion, I dove, crawled, and ended in a strange position by the couch, away from the door as it opened.

Mommy looked at me. "Is this a new kind of stretch for dance or something?"

I considered. I was at the foot of our sofa, my legs were bent in the air with my back somewhat arched on the floor.

"Yes," I answered. "This is the cricket stretch we do in contemporary class." It was a lie, but they didn't know.

My father walked over and looked down at me. "Rise, my cricket. We have some news."

I sat up straight. "News, what news?"

My mommy and daddy looked at each other.

My father said, "With the new baby coming in a few months, we've decided to move to a larger home. Because Grandma Jen is getting older, she'll be moving in with us as well."

"Larger?" I raised one eyebrow, a trick I recently learned from the otherwise Stupid Sean Hanner. "How much larger than the apartment?"

Daddy smiled like he was an evil prince with a secret. "Much larger. Put on your shoes, and let's go see."

I jumped up and ran to the front door and started pulling on my Sketcher sneakers. "Does this mean you two made up?"

Mommy and Daddy looked at each other. Mommy said, "It means that we thought we could put the argument on hold," at the same time Daddy said, "You don't need to worry about us."

I'm so glad they seem to have made up!

Warmly,

Miss W

PS

I'll tell you about the houses in the next letter.

Dear the Man Upstairs,

It is now the day after we went house-hunting. I wrote you the last letter late at night, underneath my covers, with a flashlight, on a hardcover copy of a biology book about puberty called *It's Perfectly Normal*. Spoiler alert: apparently all the changes my body is going through and will go through are perfectly normal. Yeah, no kidding. I mean Mommy doesn't look like me, so I knew I'd have to change at some point. All the weird stuff won't happen until I'm in sixth grade, though. Anyways, now I'm writing to you on our tiny kitchen table.

Yesterday, I put on my shoes, went down the elevator that always creaks when it passes the third floor, and skipped out to our car with Mommy and Daddy. We stopped by Grandma Jen's brick condo, and Mommy texted her. Grandma Jen came out in a nice blue dress, yellow bag, and a clipboard. She got into our Honda minivan and Dad was all like, "Mom, what's with the clipboard?"

Grandma Jen said, "Oh, Cameron. Don't you know you get a better price if you seem unhappy? I'll just ask some questions and then write stuff down and make 'em sweat. It'll be fun."

Daddy said, "If you say so."

Mommy said, "Of course, she does. She always gets the last say," but it was in a tone I think was meant to be sarcastic.

Grandma Jen said, "That's right, dear."

The first house we went to was two stories with white paint and a red-tiled roof. The inside was kind of like too shiny, all wooden floors and polished rails for the polished stairs, and shiny almost marble counters next to a shiny metal refrigerator in a shiny, unused kitchen. Mommy and Daddy went to go look around and yell at each other quietly, so I decided to do my own thing. I took off my shoes and tried to see just how slide-y the shiny floors were. Sometimes, with socks and slippery floors, I can do crazy flexible splits. After a while, when I was still stretching, I could clearly hear the conversation between the uptight realtor lady and my grandmother.

Grandma Jen said, "And are the windows Italian?" The realtor paused for a moment. I got out of my splits and army-crawled behind a shiny leather chair to see the scene unfold.

Grandma Jen was standing with the clipboard, pen hovering above a piece of paper.

"Um, no," the realtor said. "They're local, double paned."

Grandma Jen frowned. "I see." She wrote something down. "Well, thank you. We'll be in touch." Grandma Jen walked toward the front door, Mommy and Daddy following behind her.

"Well, come along now, dear," she said, turning around and motioning me to come out from my hiding place.

When we got back into the car I said, curiously, "What did you write down?"

Grandma Jen turned over her clipboard. "What I was feeling at that moment: goodness, what I wouldn't do for some tea."

Mommy looked like she was gripping the steering wheel so hard her knuckles were turning white.

The next house was better, and that is an understatement. It was something that Grandma Jen said Grandpa Claude would have liked. According to Daddy, he would have said it was "better than a sharp stick in the eye kind of good," because that's something Grandpa Claude said a lot.

The house was near my school, which has big advantages. For example, I could walk to school. Then I wouldn't have to hear Mommy complain about driving me everywhere, and she would get so much more free time. Daddy also saw this as a good thing.

He said, when I was getting out of the car and so he thought I was out of earshot, "Karen, if we move here, you won't spend so much time schlepping everywhere, and you really could get a job."

Mom started to say something like, "But I'll still have to take her to Dr. Keaty, and that's a far—" but I couldn't hear the rest because Grandma Jen looked at me with arms crossed and one eyebrow raised, and I knew it was time to move away from the spy-work I was doing. With her eyebrows like that, she looked like Stupid Sean Hanner, and so I ran up to her and said, "You look like Stupid Sean Hanner like that."

Grandma Jen looked back at me. "Sean Hanner seems pretty smart."

"Yes, he *seems* that way. But he isn't, at least, not really."

Then Grandma Jen said, "Well, in that case, use stronger language. Like 'Insipid Sean Hanner,' 'Vapid Sean Hanner,' maybe even 'Significantly Lacking in the Brains Department Sean Hanner.' You have lots of choices."

I took her hand and walked up the short, flower-lined steps to the dark wood front door. "Thanks, Grandma. But I'm a girl who sticks with her own insults."

Grandma Jen smiled. "Whatever floats your boat."

The inside of the house was everything a girl could dream of. It was more of a castle than a house, if I'm being honest. I think it had seven bedrooms or something crazy like that.

But all over the house, Grandma Jen was walking, and putting stuff down on her clipboard, and the realtor man was hovering behind her with his hands knotted together. Dr. Keaty told me that knotted fists are a sign of anxiety, so I hope the guy was alright. Grandma Jen can be pretty intense. Anyways, as we were done touring, Grandma Jen said, "And I assume all the paint of the interior is hypoallergenic, carbon free, and non-GMO?"

The realtor looked quite confused. "I could look into that for you. I assure you, all the paint we use is completely safe and healthy. We use the gold standard of paint, if you will."

Grandma Jen pursed her lips. "I see. Logical." She wrote something down. "Well, we appreciate your hard work. I'm sure you'll fix up the floors in no time." We walked out. I asked her back in the car, "What was wrong with the floors?"

"Nothing." Then she winked. "But he's gonna spend all day trying to figure it out."

Mommy muttered, "I'm going to spend all day wondering why exactly I agreed to living with you."

Daddy said, "Karen!" in the same voice he uses whenever Daddy gets too annoyed at me to keep ignoring me and yells, "Miss W! Stop that right now!" Mommy glared at Daddy and stopped talking to him for the rest of the car ride.

The last house we visited was also in walking distance of my school. I don't love Nelson Elementary, but I do love walking. If we moved there, I bet I could run to school and get out some energy before the school day started. Then I might be able to sit still for first period and complete the "attentive" part of my fifth-grade readiness checklist.

This last house wasn't as big as the second one (though I'm not sure any house I've ever seen was that big) or even the first one. It was pretty normal looking, wooden, painted a kind of red-brown color, with a garage and two stories. It smelled really good, though, like the house was baking bread. (It later turned out that there was bread baking in the oven, and so I felt very proud of my nose. I could be like one of those dogs at the airport and sniff out bad guys.)

I spent the first few minutes of the tour staring out one of the living room windows and watching an old man try to drag along his dog on a leash. The old man looked like one of those scientists in those videos Mrs. N liked to show us, you know the ones where there's an old guy in a white coat acting like he's younger than a kindergartner but using really big words? That's what this guy reminded me of. He had this small white fluffy puppy that had first gone over to someone's front yard, then it ran to the driveway of another house, and suddenly it just sat down in the middle of the street and refused to move. The old dude kept pulling but the dog didn't budge. Finally, the man let out a sigh (a visible sigh!) and walked over to his puppy and then lifted the dog up into his arms and started walking away.

The house has one big problem: it only has three bedrooms. I might have to share a room with my little sister once she comes along. I don't want to share a room. Room-sharing is hard. Nina says she loves her little sister, but sometimes she has to tickle her as punishment for being annoying. Then she says, "You're so lucky you have your own room." I've never had to tickle someone before so I'm not sure I'll know how.

As we were leaving, Grandma Jen asked the realtor, "Is this home disaster prepared?"

"Absolutely," the realtor said. "The roof is sturdy and should last you in a tornado. The foundation even makes the home safe for most earthquakes."

"Oh, most earthquakes. It'll just fall apart for the big and actually dangerous ones. Ah, but never mind. When was that roof reinforced or built?"

The realtor paused. "The home was remodeled just last year."

Grandma Jen pursed her lips. "Last year? Oh, dear. All those chemicals are still fresh then." She walked out the door, Mommy and I close behind, and Daddy still looking around. "Well, come along now, Cameron."

And that was how my first day of summer went. Ooh I hope we move to the second house with all the bedrooms.

Sincerely,

Miss W

PS

Isn't Grandma Jen just too cool? I worry that maybe she's also a little bit mean, but what do you think?

Dear the Man Upstairs,

After we got home, Daddy said, "I'm calling a family meeting." He wants to move soon and be all settled by the new school year, which only gives us three months.

Grandma Jen said, "Well, isn't that just funny, Cameron, because here I am with my family, and I think we're already having a meeting."

Daddy frowned and I thought, *Oh, yeah, even if he seems all big and grown up and stuff with me, he's just as much of a kid as I am to Grandma Jen, except I am super mature and I can have woman to woman conversations with Grandma, so maybe in her eyes, I'm more of an adult.*

I don't know how Grandma Jen feels about Mommy, but I think I know how Mommy feels about Grandma Jen. Mommy sometimes says that Grandma Jen's heart is in the right place, but she should just keep her head out of my "differences." She only says this to Daddy, though, but sometimes I hear things. I wish my mom and grandma got along better.

After Grandma Jen noticed we were already in a family meeting, we sat down on our plush couch. I slouched so my feet would touch the floor. In a few years, I'll be able to sit straight and not even swing my knees.

Daddy asked, "Which house was your favorite, Mom?"

Grandma Jen said, "Let's get Karen's opinion, since I am sure it will be the strongest." This was a bad idea, because Mommy gets stuck once she decides something, but you can help her decide something you want if you make her wait a little and listen. But it all worked out because then Mommy said, "Let's listen to my daughter."

This was very good, because I had something to say. "I like the second house the best!"

Daddy laughed, and Grandma Jen made that face she makes when a little kid falls down and their Mommy is on their phone, and Mommy hit Daddy and then Daddy said, "Ow."

Mommy said, "I thought your father was going to tell you, but we just went to the second house for fun, sweetie. It's out of our price range. We were seeing what we might want in a few years down the line."

I realized that I wouldn't get my dream house. The beautiful balcony and my little sister's room, and the walk-in closets were all never going to happen. I would have to share a room with a baby, and I'd never be able to sleep at all, and I hate it, I hate it, I hate it!

And then Daddy said, "Do you have a preference between the first or the third home?"

I couldn't even answer the question. I couldn't really hear anything. It just felt like everything was *too* much all of a sudden, and I ran to my room. It took me a second to realize I was crying.

I heard Mommy yell, "Cameron, I need to talk to you in our room, right now!"

I heard a shuffling of steps, and I imagined that Mommy was opening the door to my parents' bedroom and standing up with all of her five feet and three inches and *glaring* at Daddy with her hair just as red as mine.

I heard Grandma Jen say, "Real nice, son, real nice. You could've just told her what was possible, and she would've had a blast looking at houses and she wouldn't be crying."

Mommy said, "You can't even be bothered to come to a simple school meeting and now this? What are you *doing*, Cameron?"

Daddy said, "Calm down, Karen."

"Don't you dare tell me to calm down. Don't you dare." Mommy's voice shook.

"Okay, I won't. I'm sorry," Daddy said.

Mommy made a noise in the back of her throat that sounded kind of like something halfway between a laugh and a cough. "Are you? You sure don't seem that way."

Grandma Jen said, "If you two are going to argue, do it somewhere your daughter can't just wander out and see you."

I heard more shuffling, and I imagined that Daddy had his head bowed with his blond hair flopping into his eyes because he needs a haircut and then I heard Mommy slam the door to her bedroom. It was silent for a second and then I heard the door to my room open.

Grandma Jen came in and pressed a kiss to my temple. "I love you so much. I have to go to a doctor's appointment so I can't take you out today, but we'll get ice cream soon, okay?"

I hugged Mr. Wiggles, my stuffed polar bear, close to my chest. "Okay. Are Mommy and Daddy fighting because of me?"

Grandma Jen shook her head. "No, no, of course not. Don't ever think that. They just need to sort things out."

She gave Mr. Wiggles a quick kiss, too, and then left my room to go to the doctor's.

I sat on my bed all upset. I held Mr. Wiggles, and I said, "I bet that you think Daddy messed up too, huh? Just like Mommy thinks."

I wanted to hear Mommy and Daddy's conversation, so I took Mr. Wiggles into my arms for support and curled up on the floor and put my ear to the crack under my door. I felt kind of like a superspy, except I don't think what I heard will be very interesting to the CIA.

Mommy told Daddy how bad of a father he is, and he told her that wasn't fair, and after that she said that setting expectations had never been Daddy's strong suit. Daddy said that he could use some compassion, and he was trying his best.

Then Mommy said, "Are you? This is your *best,* Cameron?"

"Karen, it was just one mistake. It's not that big of a deal."

"Cameron, it's not just that you didn't tell her about the house. You always forget not just to tell her things, but to talk to her, even at all."

"That's not fair, Karen, and you know it."

"Oh, really? When was the last time you asked her about her day?"

I thought about this. Daddy never asks me about my day.

Daddy paused. "Back when she had…"

"Back when she had?" Mommy prompted.

Daddy groaned. "Back when she had that thing at her ballet studio. It's not important. What's important is that I put food on the table. I'd like at least a little credit for that."

"And you have it. Thanks for all you do, Cameron. But it's not like you being the one with the job makes you a good parent."

It sounded like Daddy slammed his hands into the wall. "Karen, I work long hours. I understand that you have responsibilities, too, but it's not as if my job makes me any less of a father. If anything, I put more into our daughter than you."

Mommy was silent for a moment. "Do you know what the school told me at the start of this year?" I leaned in closer to make sure I heard. Mommy had started talking more quietly like she does when she's unhappy or about to cry, which I've only ever seen four times.

"What, Karen?" Daddy asked like he does when I tug at his shirt sleeve.

"The school said that in light of my daughter's behavior in class, she needed to see a professional, and that they were considering moving her to special ed to accommodate her learning issues. I was told I needed to fix my daughter by winter break, or she would be moved into an entirely new program. All the jumping and energy and brightness needed to be fixed. You know I've brought her to so many meetings with Dr. Keaty, taken so many calls from Mrs. N, gone in to the counselor and dealt with almost everything on my own. Even just last week, I was all on my own, and I appreciate that you have a job, and you support us, but I thought we were raising a child together, and I've just been so alone." She sniffled and then she said, almost muffled, like there was something stuck in her throat, "Cameron, when was the last time you asked me about *my* day?"

I took my ear away from the door. It wasn't that I wasn't curious to see how Daddy would respond, but just then I felt like I didn't want to hear anymore. I wish I hadn't heard anything at all. Mommy is trying to do her best for me, but I didn't realize how hard I was. I guess she really spends a lot of time talking to my teachers and bringing me to specialists, and I have a Dr. Keaty, but no one but me in my class does. Their parents only drive them home or to after-school programs. They don't need a doctor to help them with strategies or to meet a checklist for fifth grade. I cuddled Mr. Wiggles close to my chest.

"I'm a little excitable, and I can't stay still sometimes, but you love me all the same, right?" But Mr. Wiggles is a stuffed animal, and he can't say anything. I hated that he couldn't do anything for me, so I threw him as hard as I could across the room. Throwing something felt good, and I picked up my sneaker and almost threw that, too, but then I remembered what Dr. Keaty said. "When you need to move, move, but do it safely. Maybe try doing some ballet if you can." And so with a little bit of water in my eyes, and Mr. Wiggles wedged behind a pile of clothing and the wall, I put my hand on the corner of my desk, and I began doing pliés.

I hope tomorrow will be better,
Miss W

Dear the Man Upstairs,

Mommy and Daddy were still mad at each other in the morning after the big fight about me and the houses and Daddy not being clear with me. I brought Mr. Wiggles with me to breakfast for some cuddles and normally Mommy would say, "No stuffed animals at the table," which goes along with her rules "no singing at the table," "no leg-swinging at the table," and the biggest of all, "no drumming at the table."

But Mr. Wiggles is a very sneaky bear, and Mommy was busy being mad at Daddy and didn't notice that Mr. Wiggles was sitting next to me and not drinking the orange juice that I poured for him. Mr. Wiggles likes to admire orange juice from afar.

Mommy and Daddy barely noticed me at all, so I made myself cereal. Daddy was telling Mommy, "I have a moving allowance, Karen! That's the whole reason we're able to buy a house, remember? My new job will literally pay for people to come and box our things for us."

Mommy was going red in the face. "And what if they mess everything up, did you think of that?" she yelled. "They won't understand how to preserve the oil paintings, and they'll steal my jewelry."

Daddy said, "They won't. Movers are decent people. What, is the whole world out to get you? Be reasonable."

Mommy screamed, "Be reasonable? Is it reasonable the way you've been acting? Is it unreasonable for me to want some support every once in a while?"

Daddy said, "The moving team will support you if you just ask them! Honestly, Karen, stop trying to reinvent the wheel." And then they noticed that I was sitting quietly at the table with them, eating Cheerios and swinging my legs. (Since Mommy hadn't noticed Mr. Wiggles, I thought I could break more than one rule. It was very exciting. It almost helped distract me from how much I hate it when my parents fight.)

Mommy put a hand over her eyes. "All this stress cannot be good for the baby. Cameron, please just call your mother to take our daughter for the day."

Daddy looked upset but said, "Oh, alright."

Today is a special day, so I said, "I can't go with Grandma Jen for the whole day today."

Mommy still had that hand over her eyes. "And why is that." She didn't really say it like a question, it was more flat. Dr. Keaty told me that sometimes when people are upset they can either have really strong reactions or really small ones.

I kept my voice quiet so that I wouldn't make Mommy any more upset. "I have a meeting with Dr. Keaty. We're working on our checklist for fifth grade."

Daddy said, to Mommy instead of to me, "Mom can still drive her to the appointment."

Mommy said, "She can. It's the least she can do. At least once Jen starts living with us, I won't have to take care of Miss

W all the time. Though I doubt it will be worth everything else that comes with your mother."

I wanted to tell her I could take care of myself. and I was fine, and that Grandma Jen is worth *everything,* but it didn't seem like the time to say anything. Instead, I hugged Mr. Wiggles close to my chest because I at least take care of *him* and waited for Grandma Jen to come and pick me up.

When she buzzed to get into the apartment, Mommy didn't let her in and instead sent me out into the hallway, Mr. Wiggles and all. I rode down the elevator all by myself.

When I got into the lobby, Grandma Jen raised an eyebrow at my companion. "I'll have to start charging you if you bring any more uninvited guests into my vehicle."

I told her, "I don't have money, but I can pay you in hugs."

Grandma Jen smiled. "Well, then, I might charge interest." She took my hand and led me out to her car.

Dr. Keaty was surprised to see Grandma Jen instead of Mommy, but we had our meeting all the same.

We've been working on sitting still for a while now, and I still have some struggles. We've learned that if I use a fidget toy, I can focus on reading for longer than I can without a fidget.

Dr. Keaty is hoping she'll be able to convince the school that I meet the expectations for fifth-grade behavior and that the fidget toy is the opposite of distracting. It might depend on my teacher, though, because Mr. Odber seems nice, but Ms. Langies is supposed to be terrible. Terrence Greenberg, Nina's older brother's best friend, told me that Ms. Langies is a dragon lady who likes to eat her young. I think that Terrence was using a metaphor, but I still think it makes Ms. Langies seem scary.

After the meeting with Dr. Keaty, Grandma Jen reminded me that it was July eleventh. July eleventh is the anniversary of Grandpa Claude's death. Every July eleventh, Grandma Jen, Daddy, and I all go to the cemetery and bring Grandpa Claude cannoli.

Grandma Jen always says on July eleventh that Grandpa Claude loved cannoli and sunsets and being outside even when normal people were inside.

We always go to the cemetery right before dusk (and I get to stay up past my bedtime) and then Grandma Jen will lay down a bunch of yarrow on Grandpa Claude's stone and trim back the weeds, and we'll sit together as the sky goes pink.

I asked her if we should go and pick up Daddy before we went to the cemetery, and she said no because if Daddy forgot what day it was, maybe that was a good thing. "Grief comes in all shapes and sizes and sometimes I think your dad's grief is three sizes too big."

Grandpa Claude died way before I was born, and before Daddy met Mommy. He died when Daddy was fifteen and Uncle Mathias was seventeen. I've only met Uncle Mathias twice because he and Grandma Jen don't talk anymore, but sometimes someone besides Daddy and Grandma Jen and me leaves flowers for Grandpa Claude so we know Uncle Mathias has been by. (He lives in California though, so it's not very often.)

Grandma Jen bought cannoli while I was with Dr. Keaty, so we drove to the cemetery together right after the appointment, and this time, I bent down to pick the weeds because Grandma Jen's knees are getting old. Then we watched the sky go all pink sitting on the same ratty purple blanket Grandma Jen always brings on July eleventh.

We stayed until the stars came out, and then Grandma Jen said, "You know, he met me at a planetarium."

I said, "Grandpa Claude met you at a planetarium?"

"He told me after the show to make a wish on a falling star, and I told him that I didn't see any. We were inside this little museum, after all. He had this god-awful sticker of the big dipper in his hand and dropped it right in front of me and then said, with his cheeky little grin, 'Would you look at that, a couple falling stars just for you.'"

Grandma Jen doesn't talk about Grandpa Claude much and never about how he died.

I asked her, "What was he like?"

And she said, "That's a story for another time."

I didn't really know what to say, so I just settled for giving Grandma Jen a hug. She didn't say anything else for a long while.

As we were packing up to go back home, Daddy came by. We were standing up and about to head back to the car, and he walked past us and kneeled down by Grandpa Claude's stone. He looked really sad, and I almost went to give *him* a hug, but Grandma Jen stopped me.

She said, "I think we best let him have some alone time with his father."

And so right before we left, Daddy gave me a small smile and said, "See you back at the ranch in a few minutes, champ."

The last thing I heard him say before his voice was drowned out by the wind was, "Hey, Dad, it's been a while."

Sincerely,

Miss W

PS

I know you and my Grandma Jen are friends, but did you know Grandpa Claude? I know almost nothing about him. And do you know my little brother? Please let me know.

Dear Miss W,

As a matter of fact, I did know your grandfather. He used to call himself a friend of "that good, old, bearded man who lives in the sky," which was his nickname for me. I never met your little brother in any way that mattered, but I know that he and your grandfather love each other very much and are spending a lot of time together above the clouds.

Claude didn't much care for me when he was a teenager and spent a lot of time pretending I didn't exist, but he came around a little after he graduated from high school. I don't know everything about him and his childhood, but I do know some important details.

He had two younger sisters and one younger brother. He used to tell me that he was glad he'd been born a boy because his younger sister, Eva, had to help a lot with diaper changing and taking care of baby Leah and then baby Joel. Because he was the oldest boy, Claude was supposed to be responsible, and he got his first job when he was eight as one of the newspaper boys. He was one of the kids who would always wake up early no matter how tired he was and how late he stayed up, so he loved being a paperboy.

Claude would always tell me that if he could go back and relive any time in his life, he'd relive those morning bike rides. I know that in middle school, he began swimming with a team and that he worked in a movie theater.

His cafeteria had cookies you could buy for a nickel, and a lot of kids would forget to bring money with them. Claude always had a lot of change on him, and he would tell his class-mates that he would lend them a nickel, but then they would owe him a dime.

So many kids wanted a cookie right then and would agree. And the next day, he would ask them, "Where's my dime?"

He was pretty big from all the swimming, and he was also nice and dependable and almost everyone paid him back. He would never lend someone another nickel until they paid him back, and a lot of kids liked relying on being able to get a nickel if they forgot their money at home. After he made enough money, he would bring his little siblings to this hole-in-the-wall Italian restaurant in their neighborhood and buy them cannoli.

I think he kept doing it throughout high school. His junior year he really wanted a car, and he got a job at the planetarium in this tiny science museum in his neighborhood. I believe that's where he met your grandmother.

She didn't like him at first. Your grandmother was a bit stuck-up back in the day. They were both great parents. Claude was the best father he could be in the years he had with both his sons.

But enough about Claude. Have your parents thought of any baby names for your little sister? Have you? Somehow, I feel like you might have some opinions. Will you keep seeing Dr. Keaty next year?

Looking forward to our next letter,
the Man Upstairs

Dear the Man Upstairs, AKA "That good old bearded old man who lives in the sky,"

It's too bad you never met my brother. I didn't either.

I have started a list of names I want the baby in Mommy's stomach to have, thank you for asking. So far, I've suggested Anthophila (the scientific name for bee), and Plätzchen (the German word for cookie.) Not enough people speak German, that's what I think. You can't learn German at Nelson Elementary. This is very sad, because Germany invented the soft pretzel, which is objectively the best food on the planet.

Anyways, neither of my names have made it into the official list of names. Right now, my mommy is stuck between Choral, Margaret, Onyx, and Elizabeth. I'm hoping for Anthophila first, but if not, I'd like to have a sister named Onyx. Dad's favorite name was Genevieve, but during the fighting, it got taken off. Daddy made dinner one night and suddenly the name Genevieve reappeared on the naming wall in the kitchen.

Daddy didn't come back for a long time after he went to visit Grandpa Claude, and I was asleep by the time he got back.

In the morning, I went to my first day at swim camp. There are no ballet classes at my studio this summer because Teacher Cindy won the lottery and decided that teaching ballet was no longer her calling. Mommy said that with the baby on the way she can't keep being my entertainment all the time.

I started swim camp with a big scary man who's actually a softy named Coach Summers the day the movers came. After practice, Grandma Jen brought me to Baskin-Robbins. We're trying to see if we can try all thirty-one flavors before the end of the summer. We have to keep the ice cream a secret, though, because Mommy has decided that sugar is bad for me and my behavior.

Dr. Keaty disagrees with Mommy and said that there was no evidence to suggest that my behaviors are in any way related to my diet, but Mommy hasn't listened and now there's no more dessert in the house. I need to ask Mommy if I'll keep seeing Dr. Keaty next school year. I hope I don't. I like Dr. Keaty, but I think it would be nice to not have to visit a doctor, you know? It makes me feel like I'm sick or there's something wrong with me, and I don't like to think that's true. I'll let you know as soon as I find out.

Mommy says she thinks her war on sugar has made a difference, but I'm still getting ice cream three times a week with Grandma Jen. I don't think it's true. Mommy is now in her third trimester, so she's started to tell everyone she's pregnant now, but I think you can kinda tell just by looking at her. I'm really relieved. Last time she didn't make it past the second trimester.

I stayed the night with Grandma Jen in her studio and everything was in boxes except one bed, which Grandma Jen and I shared. The next day we went to our new house, the third one we visited, which is bigger than my old apartment. I heard Grandma Jen say it will feel smaller once my sister comes along. I don't think I like our new house very much. My room has a window that faces the road so all I can see is gray pavement and cars, and the light in my room is so much dimmer than the light I had back in the apartment. Even Mr. Wiggles doesn't like the new house. He didn't leave my arms for the entire day.

The moving-in of our new house was not fun. Mommy and Daddy spent the morning screaming at each other over where to put the family picture we took when I was three years old. Daddy insisted it had to be in the living room, and Mommy said it needed to be in the hallway by the big window. They didn't stop fighting in the afternoon but "took a break" because "fighting is bad for the baby, Cameron. Do you want to induce labor this early?"

Grandma Jen rolled her eyes at Mommy, and then Daddy asked Grandma Jen if she had any suggestions for baby names.

Grandma Jen said, "Have a boy and name him Claude. I already got the girl name I wanted."

Daddy gave me this weird smile and said, "She is a good girl and I'm lucky to have her," before wandering away to set up his at-home office with the movers.

Grandma Jen stared after him for a long time before she came over to where I was, tucked me under her arm, and whispered, "How about we blow this popsicle stand and go get ice cream?"

I kind of liked being included in Grandma Jen's "We." It made me feel like someone was listening to me. You make me feel like that too.

Warmly,

Miss W: A Super Special Ice Cream Eater

PS

Thanks for telling me about Grandpa Claude. How did he and Grandma Jen get together?

Dear the Man Upstairs,

It's August. There are two weeks left and twenty-four more ice cream flavors to try before I go back to school. I love the summer because I can move as much as I want. I've been dancing a lot at home and also swimming a lot at camp. I like swim lessons but my coach (Coach Summers, funny, because I met him in the summer) just kept telling me to put my arm into the water at a ninety-degree angle. I didn't know what he meant so I just kept swimming and kicked my legs harder.

When I got home, I asked my daddy what Coach Summers had meant, but he was on a "very important phone call, with a super-extra-important client, who might just have some—" Anyways, he was too busy. And then I went to Mommy, but she was doing that weird thing where she watches this video and then starts rubbing lavender oil on her belly while sitting in the bathroom while the shower runs and says things like "Hi, baby. This is Ma-Ma," which honestly kind of freaks me out. Mommy's started doing this about once a week because it's something Clover, an essential oil specialist who advises all the mommies on the Facebook group, said is good for babies. It's supposed to be calming for Mommy and her baby. I think Clover might be wrong.

If I was Anthophila (which is what my sister will be named, I promise, the scientific name for bees will set her up for success), I'd just be all like "I know who you are, Mommy, and I'm just going to stay in your stomach because you are a scary woman, and I know I'm safe inside."

I asked Grandma Jen, who lives with us now, and she told me that a ninety-degree angle is a line parallel to the floor. I asked what parallel meant, which is two lines just the same but apart, does that make sense?

Anyways, to answer your question from a few days ago, I will keep seeing Dr. Keaty next year. I asked Mommy if I'd keep seeing Dr. Keaty in fifth grade, and she said something like I'll keep seeing Dr. Keaty until I'm eighteen. I asked if I would be all better when I'm eighteen and Mommy said no, but then I'll need a doctor for adults to help fix me.

That felt mean somehow and made me want to curl up into a little ball. Do you think I need to be fixed?

Grandma Jen was in the kitchen making herself two egg whites with one tablespoon of maple syrup, which is all she eats for breakfast, every day, except sometimes she has oatmeal too—oatmeal is so gross—but anyways, Grandma Jen stopped making her breakfast and came over. She took my face in her hands and said, "Now, look you here, there is nothing wrong with you, and nothing that needs to be better. You just need some strategies."

I started to say, "I know—"

But then Mommy said, "Jennifer, she knows that. I'm not saying anything is wrong with her."

Grandma Jen walked over and patted Mommy on the cheek. "You just worry your little head over that baby of yours on the way, and I'll take care of this baby of mine." Then Grandma Jen pulled at my hand and said, "Let's go get us some ice cream."

But then Mommy pulled at my arm and said, "And where were you when my daughter was called into the office? Who brings her to Dr. Keaty? Who helped her all last year when the school wanted to put her in special ed? Who is talking to the school over the summer to keep her in the regular fifth grade? Is that you, Jennifer? Or is that me, her *mother*?"

Grandma Jen said, "I know you've had a hard time. I don't mean to take that away from you." And then she tried to pull me, but Mommy put her hand around my waist and pulled me close and didn't let me go.

Mommy said, "No more ice cream. Sugar isn't good for children like her. You should know that. I sent you the packet of allowed foods."

I started to say that if anyone asked me, I like ice cream, and what were my "allowed foods," and could I have all foods be allowed because I like choices, please and thank you. And what does "like her" mean?

"You're being ridiculous," Grandma Jen said.

Mommy glared at Grandma Jen. "How dare you? Do you hear yourself talk? You're so condescending all the time for no reason. I'm doing my best to keep my child happy and healthy, and it's not my fault you don't understand basic science."

Grandma Jen put her hands on her hips, and her eyebrows went to straight into her hair. She looked like she was holding back from hitting something. She exploded, "There's no science behind all your rules, Karen! You're inventing things left and right, and for what? So you can complain to other expecting mothers on the internet? So you can control your daughter? Nothing is wrong with ice cream, Karen! It's just food. FOOD is an important part of a balanced diet. Not that you'd know anything about that though, would you? You need to eat more, too—all those vegetables aren't going to be enough for you."

Mommy's green eyes flashed, and she pressed her lips together before taking a deep breath and shouting, "You don't get it! I lost a baby! I can't...I can't...I *can't* do that again. I can't...I can't keep doing this. You just push, and push, and you think you get it and know better than me. You think that it's, what, perfectly fine for you to sit behind me when I'm playing bridge with my *friends* and belittle me, but you can't stand it when I parent my own child? You're not a saint, Jen. I'm the mother here, and I'm saying no. You will not take her out to ice cream, and you will respect the rules of my house."

"Oh, so it's your house? Do you think I just pay a third of the property taxes and mortgage for fun? This is just as much my house as yours, and I want to take my granddaughter to get ice cream."

"I said no!"

"I don't care!"

Mommy and Grandma Jen kept arguing with each other, and I tried to pull my wrists free from both of their grasps because it hurt a little. I didn't want to be there in that kitchen because I was scared, and they were fighting. I hate it when they fight and yell. It makes me want to cover my ears and—

Grandma Jen was about to say something, but Daddy, who was working in his new office, came into the kitchen saying, "Please be quiet," and then he saw what was happening and said, firmly, "You both need to let go of my daughter right now."

Mommy and Grandma Jen both looked at where they were holding me and seemed to notice for the first time that I was pulling away. Grandma Jen let go first and then Mommy did, too, and I immediately backed up a bunch of steps.

Daddy shook his head. "Don't fight in front of the kid. Isn't that what you said, Mom?" He gave me a wink. "What do you say we get out of here while they work this out?"

I nodded furiously. "Yes, please."

Grandma Jen and Mommy were so shocked, they didn't say anything. I can't remember the last time I did something with Daddy, just the two of us.

Daddy brought me outside, and we got into his fancy Lexus which he never lets me ride in, and we went to Auntie Anne's to get a soft pretzel because he knows I love those. He never talked once about what had happened until we were driving home.

Then he said, "They both love you, you know. They're both trying to do what's right."

And then I said, "I know," because that's what Mommy says to Daddy, but I didn't really know. So I asked, "What is right, Daddy?"

And then we were home, and he sat in the driveway and unbuckled his seatbelt and gave me a real big hug. He kissed the top of my head and said, "I don't know, champ. I don't know."

So I'll ask you, Man Upstairs, what is right?

Sincerely,

Miss W

Dear the Man Upstairs,

Coach Summers called Mommy up yesterday because I go back to school in four days, so today was my last day of practice. He told Mommy that I have "real potential" and that he'd "like to see me on his team outside of camp," which is super cool.

I decided to keep swimming next year and quit dance, because I'm not going to be a bee no matter what I do, and I love swimming and being on a team.

Mommy had to take me to Dr. Keaty this morning so we could keep working on the checklist for fifth grade readiness. We have to work on six things together: directions and rules, attention, collaboration, performance, time control, behavior, and emotion. Today we worked on directions and time management.

Dr. Keaty gave me a really large packet of paper. "This is a test. This test has fifty questions. I need you to do as much of the test as you can in thirty minutes. If you don't know the answer to something, leave it blank and move on. Read every direction on the test before starting to answer questions."

I said, "Yes, Dr. Keaty," because we've been working together on the "behavior" part of the checklist, which is all about respecting the other students, teachers, and myself. Saying "Yes, Dr. Keaty," is polite, and being polite is a good thing that all fifth graders should try to be.

When I first got the packet, it was a little overwhelming. I really wanted to just not take the test and run around outside. It took me almost three minutes to even try to read the directions at the top of the test, and by then, all the words looked like scribbles and dripping ice cream and then I remembered I was hungry.

The test told me to read every test question before answering any of them, but I thought that maybe that would be a waste of time because I only had thirty minutes to answer fifty questions, which meant I had less than a minute to answer every question. I couldn't waste time reading *every single* question's directions before answering them!

The first question of the test read: *Who is the patron saint of Ireland?*

Mommy is Irish, so I'm half Irish, but I didn't know. I was confused by "patron saint." I didn't know what that meant. I looked at the question as if that would make it easier for me to answer it, but I gave up and went on to the next one.

The next question read: *What country is responsible for the creation of the Olympic games?*

I didn't know that one either.

The next question was: *How many eyes do bees have?*

I smiled at this one because I knew the answer! I wrote *five* and felt like maybe this test wasn't so hard after all.

I was wrong.

The next question seemed even harder than the first two: *Name the former country that bordered fourteen nations and crossed eight time zones.*

I had to take a deep breath and blink my eyes really fast. I didn't know that one either! I looked at the clock. It had been eleven minutes, and I was only on question four. I'd only answered one question. It felt like everything was going wrong.

That feeling only got worse as the test went on and the questions got harder. By question fifteen, I barely understood what I was reading. Question fifteen asked me to find a derivative of some other number, and I had no idea what that meant. That question made me frown and bite the inside of my cheek because I was so confused.

I read question twenty aloud to Dr. Keaty, "An eye for an eye makes the whole world blind is a common saying. The current American Judi-si-Judi—"

I showed her the word, and she said, "Judicial, it means legal or approved by the courts."

I just nodded because I had a feeling the rest of the question would be harder, and I continued, "Okay, so the current American Judicial system incarse... incarsa—"

"Incarcerates," Dr. Keaty said. "It means put in jail or prison. Do you think maybe you should move on to the next question?"

I didn't want to move on because there was so much more to the question, and it had been twenty-two minutes and I had still only answered the question about the bee. The words were swimming again, and I felt this feeling growing in my stomach like I was going really quickly down a hill. I had this terrible image of me crashing into a wall and crumpling up. I felt like I *needed* to answer this question to prove something—that I could do it maybe—but Dr. Keaty was right. I didn't know any of the words in the question and so I had to move on.

But moving on was terrible because each question was impossible for me to figure out. I couldn't understand any of the words. I found myself getting more and more frustrated. Dr. Keaty was just sitting happy as can be at her desk as I tried to work through problems I could not possibly understand. I started pulling out my hair and looking at the clock. Twenty-eight minutes had passed, I was on question thirty-four, and I had left every single question blank except for question three.

I gnawed on my lips and thought about what I could try to do. It felt like this was it: I was never going to finish this test, I was never going to be able to get into fifth grade, and I would spend the rest of my life in a doctor's office pretending that maybe I might get a future even though I know in the back of my head that I won't.

It felt like the office was disappearing, and I heard the sound of the clock ticking through a tunnel. I felt like I couldn't breathe and that my heart was beating out of my chest. All I could think was, *I'm never going to fifth grade, I'm never going to fifth grade*, on repeat.

Dr. Keaty's gentle voice broke me out of my freak-out. "Breathe, Miss W. Come on now, breathe with me."

Dr. Keaty took an exaggerated breath, puffing out her shoulders to show me when to breathe. I copied her, and she smiled. "Good, inhale big and strong." I took a deep breath. "And now exhale, long and strong." I let it out. "Good," she repeated. "Well done."

I breathed with Dr. Keaty for maybe about two minutes before I said, "I don't know any of these."

Dr. Keaty leveled me with a stare, "And what do we do when we're confused?"

I thought about all our work together, "Regroup, and see what we do know. And then, if we need to, ask for help."

She gave me an encouraging nod, and I went back to looking at the test. The top of the test still said, "Read every question in this test before answering any of them." Feeling like I had nothing left to lose, I did that. The questions were all still confusing until I got to question forty-two. Question forty-two read, *Go to the end of this test and draw a smiley face.*

Question forty-three said, *This is not a question.*

In fact, every single question between question forty-three and question forty-nine said, *This is not a question.*

Question fifty's direction read, *Draw a smiley face. This is the only question you need to complete.*

I drew a smiley face. It couldn't be that easy. I peered up at Dr. Keaty, who looked back at me very calmly. I looked at the clock and realized it had been forty-six minutes. It had taken me sixteen minutes too long to finish the test.

"Are you done?" Dr. Keaty asked me.

"Yes," I said quietly.

Dr. Keaty took the packet from me and flipped to the last page. "It's a very good smiley face."

"Was that really all I needed to do?" I felt a little embarrassed about how long it had taken me to figure it out. "Just draw a smiley face?" I felt a little angry too.

"There's nothing small about reading every direction carefully. You'll know for next time, won't you?"

It didn't really make me feel better, but maybe that wasn't the point. After Dr. Keaty's appointment was over, Mommy said that she wanted, "to go somewhere special, just the two of us."

I wanted to go home, but Mommy looked serious, and I thought it was better to do what she wanted. I was tired already from the meeting with Dr. Keaty, but I always have energy because that's just who I am.

Mommy took me out to the Juice Kitchen, which is a juice restaurant in Milwaukee. I got a strawberry lemonade, which was pretty okay, but it was all organic, so it tasted too healthy, and Mommy got this thing called purple haze, which tasted just awful.

After we got our juices, Mommy said, "Let's go on a walk."

I said, "No, it's hot outside," because it was.

Mommy said, "This is nonnegotiable," and I was about to disagree but then I thought about how walking in the heat can be okay. I wouldn't be antsy, plus I had a cold drink, and

Mommy says arguing is bad for my baby sister's energy. Will it still be bad after she's born?

I said, "Okay."

Mommy had us just walk around in a big circle on the sidewalks, and she was quiet for a little bit. Then she said, "You know that before I had you, I worked as an interior designer, right?"

I said, "Yes, your company was called Inside the Cover."

Mommy nodded. "Well, after you, I stopped the business to be a mommy. And I think that it was hard for me, to stop working. It was a part of me. I put everything I had into you, and then this last year. Well, you know."

"I've been too hard, right?" I know Mommy hates my need for some extra help, and it's been really challenging for her. Sometimes Grandma Jen tries to tell me Mommy is just confused, but it still makes me sad. Mommy put her hand on her belly, like she was comforting my baby sister. I thought she should have comforted me.

"No, not hard. Just different. I still love you. Even so, I want to be better with your sister, and I've been talking to Clover, and he says I should cleanse all the bad energy before I bring a new life into the world."

I just said, "Okay, Mommy," because whenever she talks about Clover, she gets super weird.

"So, I just want you to know that I love you and care about you, even if you aren't like every other kid."

I replied, "And I just want you to know that I love you, even though all the other moms I know go to real doctors and have therapists." (I heard about this from Grandma Jen and Daddy talking a few nights ago, and I didn't like Mommy calling me different. I know it wasn't very nice, but nobody is *very* nice all of the time).

Mommy was very quiet after that, and on the drive back home, she said, "I love you, even though you are different. I think that sometimes your difference is a strength because I don't know any rising fifth graders as strong as you."

That made me feel like I was glowing. "Thank you, and one day, if you want to go back to working, I'll take care of Anthophila."

Mommy said, "That's not going to be her name."

I said, "Yes, yes, it will be. And you'll love her, anyway, just like how you love me."

Sincerely,

Anthophila's Big Sister, Miss W

Dear the Man Upstairs,

The summer has ended, and Mommy still loves me, but I've gone back to school. I did well enough on the checklist that Dr. Keaty convinced the school to keep me out of special ed! I get to stay with my friends, and I am so, so happy. I got put in Ms. Langies's class with Momo but without Nina, but I have survived my first week of school, anyway. Stupid Sean Hanner and Yvette Guiteau are both in my class. Yvette has gotten taller and meaner compared to last year. She has a cute little hand-sanitizer bottle that looks like a panda in her backpack and whenever I pass by her, she pulls it out and puts it on her hand so she can't "catch" whatever I have. Every time she does that, a couple of kids laugh, and I wonder why I work so hard to go to school if it's just going to be like this all the time. Sometimes, I wish that I could be sick so I could stay home. Yvette told me that her mom argued that I should be moved into special ed and that I don't deserve to be in the regular class with "*normal* kids."

My teacher, Ms. Langies, who Nina's older brother Todd calls the dragon lady, probably agrees. I think part of Ms. Langies's problem is that she is too young to be teaching. Grandma Jen said that she "has no business in the business of education until she is old enough to be considered educated herself."

Mommy tried defending Ms. Langies, saying, "Age isn't everything, you know." But then Mommy needed to go and get away because the "potential of conflict creates a toxic energy" and that is bad for the baby. I'm really glad my sister is being born soon because it seems like everything is bad energy nowadays. Even my room being messy causes waves of badness, so Mommy makes me keep my door closed always, no exceptions, from now until Anthophila is born. Mommy lost my baby brother last time in the second trimester but we're already in the third trimester. I think that Anthophila is safe now, and bad energy is probably not going to hurt her. I don't know for certain, though, and it's probably something better safe than sorry, right?

Ms. Langies yells a lot. She likes to tell everyone in the class that we're too old to be acting so badly, and that she is very disappointed in us. After school the second day, Daddy said, "Pure and utter nonsense. In order for your teacher to be disappointed, she would need to have good expectations of you all first and have communicated them properly."

So far, Ms. Langies has sent me out of class every day because I'm having a hard time sitting still. Like on the first day of school, I kept getting up to go to the window when she wasn't talking, because Mrs. N had told me to move around when it wasn't disruptive. Ms. Langies sent me out of the classroom. Then on the second day, I started bouncing in my seat, which was disruptive, and I got sent out of the class. On the third day, I was swinging my legs, but I had a really hard time concentrating on our spelling worksheet, and I didn't finish it in time. She said I wasn't trying and sent me out of the class. Yesterday, I ran in the hallway when we were coming back from music class with Mr. Romero, and she made walk back and do it again. I did do it again, but I thought she meant she wanted me to do what I had done before exactly, so I ran again, and I guess she meant come back but not running. She yelled a lot about how I was the most disrespectful child she has ever taught (not that bad, because she's only been teaching for two years. According to Daddy, I'm the worst child out of about ninety, which isn't that disrespectful, if you ask him or Grandma Jen. Mommy wasn't in the conversation because my behavior is full of negative energy.)

Yesterday, Stupid Sean Hanner decided to be pretty smart because he finally yelled at Ms. Langies after Ms. Langies told me that my grammar was bad because I write too many run-on sentences. "Why are you being so mean? She's trying her best, you know."

Yvette Guiteau said, "Well, maybe her best isn't good enough. I don't think she should be in our class."

I said, using my best respectful voice because I need to respect my classmates, "That's not very nice."

Ms. Langies sent both Stupid Sean Hanner and me to the office, which I knew was going to be a problem because I've been sent to the office a whole lot. Sean Hanner got to go back to class, and he got a lollipop, but I had to stay in the office and then my parents were called.

Mommy is on bedrest so she couldn't come, so then Daddy came into the room and sat down next to me. And Vice Principal Viceport said that this was my "sixth office visit in eight months. We were told she had completed the fifth-grade checklist, but I have to say, this is not encouraging."

I looked down at the gray carpet and bit my lip. I didn't want to leave class so soon after I did well enough to be a part of it.

Daddy's never been to the school before, and I saw his shiny leather black shoes tap against the floor. "Have you even thought to ask her why she was sent this time?"

Vice Principal Viceport sighed and asked me, "Why were you sent to the office?"

I looked up and focused on the bit of wall behind the vice principal's desk, which has a crack that looks kind of like an elbow. "Sean Hanner told Ms. Langies to stop yelling at me all the time. A girl in my class said that maybe I don't deserve to be in the class with regular kids, and then I said to her that she wasn't being very nice."

Daddy put his arm around my shoulder. Voice quiet and cold, he said, "It sounds to me like my daughter got sent to the office for being a victim of bullying. That's not very encouraging."

Stupid Sean Hanner was called back from class. Mr. Viceport asked him why he was sent to the office, and he said, "I told Ms. Langies to stop yelling at Miss W all the time. It's only been a week of school, but she's gotten mad at Miss W every day for nothing, and it's not fair. Ms. Langies plays favorites."

Then Vice Principal Viceport sent Stupid Sean Hanner back to class, and I watched him and his green sweatshirt leave and wished I could leave the office too.

Vice Principal Viceport said, "In light of that information, I think it would be wrong of me to count this office visit against you, Miss W. Just try your best going forward, alright?"

I nodded and kept looking at the crack in the wall.

Daddy said, "I think that there is clearly something wrong with the way Ms. Langies is teaching. I hope that you have a conversation with her about this as well."

Vice Principal Viceport said, "I will. Perhaps it could make sense for your whole family and Miss W's doctor to have a conversation with Ms. Langies and the school to create a plan for the future."

Daddy said, "I think it would, thank you."

We went home together in his car. I like spending time with him.

Even though Ms. Langies is pretty mean, Nina and I have had three playdates over this week, so it's okay we're not in class together. Plus, because I've been kicked out of Ms. Langies's room so much, I keep on coming into Mr. Odber's room. He is Nina's teacher. I learned all about the solar system, which is better than the grammar we're learning with Ms. Langies. Mr. Odber doesn't seem to mind my addition to his class on occasion. He often laughs and says, "Well, if it isn't our red-haired addition again today." And since I don't belong to the class, I don't have a chair, and he doesn't care if I kinda just wander around.

Sincerely,

Miss W

PS

Remember my great babysitter, Amy? You know, the one I yelled at, and I thought hated me? It turns out she doesn't hate me! It's September now, and she's gone to school at the University of Michigan. She sent me a photo of the two of us hugging to remember her now that she won't be my babysitter anymore. She sent me a note that said she'll miss me. I guess that sometimes people can like me even after I behave badly. I put the framed photo right above my bed.

Dear the Man Upstairs,

It was gray and rainy when Daddy and Grandma Jen drove me to school for the meeting. Mommy couldn't come because baby Anthophila is due any day now.

Daddy grumbled, "They scheduled this at such an inconvenient time. I have a job."

Grandma Jen said, "Yes. Being a father."

I didn't say that's what Mommy said during Mommy and Daddy's fight last spring about meetings for me. After Grandma Jen said that, I could see through the rear-view mirror that Daddy looked like he had just eaten something rotten. I think he remembered Mommy's comment on his own.

When we got to school, Grandma Jen took my hand as I led her and Daddy back into the fifth-grade classroom. They had to duck under the little daisy chain the class made on Wednesday during art because one end of it had fallen down, and no one had bothered to pin it back up again. The room was dark, and rain beat down on the windows.

Ms. Langies was at the front of the room by the whiteboard and was talking to Ms. Genever, our assistant teacher. When she saw us come in, she stopped her talk and walked over to us.

"Mr. and Mrs. Williams, I assume?" Grandma Jen looked unimpressed, and Daddy was looking at his phone.

"Ms. Langies, I presume?" Grandma Jen asked.

Ms. Langies looked a little nervous. "If you'd like, we can all talk in the breakout room. Mr. Viceport is already there."

Grandma Jen nodded and squeezed my hand. We began to follow Ms. Langies to the breakout room.

"Oh, I'd prefer it if only the adults talked. It might be inappropriate to involve the student."

Grandma Jen kept a hold of my hand. "I think that she should be able to hear what your concerns are."

Ms. Langies shook her head. "I doubt you will want her to hear what I have to say."

I said, "I'd like to know. Really. Please."

Ms. Langies looked at my dad and sighed. "Her inability to follow directions is part of why we need to have this talk."

Daddy narrowed his eyes. "Right," he replied after a bit.

"But I can be quiet, promise, I won't distract anyone at all—" I started to say.

"Can you just go sit with your classmates, for me, champ?" Daddy interrupted. I looked into his eyes. His brow was furrowed, and he mouthed, "Please."

I couldn't say no to that, as much as I wanted to know everything that would happen. "Okay, Daddy." I hung my head and went to sit in morning circle with all of my classmates.

Grandma Jen and Daddy followed Ms. Langies with slow footsteps and angry expressions into the breakout room. Daddy was going to call Dr. Keaty with his iPad.

In morning circle, I shared that my favorite season was fall because of all the colors. Only Momo Tanaka, my best friend in Ms. Langies's class, had anything interesting to say. She said, "Summer is my favorite season because it is the season of *love.*"

I couldn't pay attention to anyone else. I kept digging my fingers into the blue carpet and trying to breathe deeply. I could hear Dr. Keaty in my head saying, "Breathe. Come on now, breathe in one, two, three, four. Good. Now exhale for one, two, three. Good."

It didn't help. I couldn't stop thinking about what was being said about me. What if Daddy and Grandma Jen came out of the meeting and said, "We were wrong to believe in you?" I half-convinced myself that was going to happen.

After morning circle, Ms. Langies still wasn't done talking to Grandma Jen and Daddy. I kept biting my bottom lip, and I couldn't seem to stop.

Ms. Genever had no idea what to do with us, so she told us to read quietly. That's not my strong suit. I asked her if I could just pace quietly instead, and she sort of looked at me, and said, "No, but you don't have to read at your desk."

I pretended to read words while I stretched on the floor because I can still do my splits from when I did ballet even though I'm on a swim team now. A lot of people pretended to read while they watched me, and even Ms. Genever smiled when I went into my straddle splits.

Momo came over and said, "Wow, how do you do that?" and then she got down beside me while I went on. I felt her sitting by my side, and I started being able to breathe around the stone I felt like was taking up my stomach.

Finally, Grandma Jen and Daddy came out of the meeting. I ran over to them and said, "What did you guys talk about?"

They looked at me and looked kinda confused, which seemed weird, and then Ms. Langies came out also looking confused and a little bit like she was faking a smile, and Mr. Viceport looked upset.

"Clearly, I haven't been doing the right things," Ms. Langies said to Mr. Viceport. "But I really hope you'll follow up with Dr. Keaty and look into medication for little Miss W. Otherwise, I'll have no choice but to—"

"I know," said Grandma Jen kind of loudly.

Daddy said, "We need to talk to her mother." Then Grandma Jen took my hand again and led me out of the classroom.

"Don't I have school?" I asked.

Grandma Jen shook her head.

Daddy said, "Mom—" but Grandma Jen interrupted him. She said, "Not today. We need to go talk to your mother."

"What did Ms. Langies say?"

Grandma Jen pursed her lips. "She thinks you need some medication for your behavior. She is too weak to handle you, so if you don't start acting differently, she wants to move you into special ed."

I shook my head. "But I don't want to move. I want to stay here, Grandma Jen."

"You won't. I'll make sure your Mommy does what she needs to do."

"What do I need medications for?" I asked. "I'm perfectly healthy."

Grandma Jen's expression looked pinched. "You are. You *are*. It's just…"

"Another kind of strategy," Daddy supplied. "You're going to get some help with focusing. Doesn't that sound nice?"

"But I'm okay the way I am, right?" I asked.

Daddy ran a hand though his hair and gave me a tight smile. "Of course, sweetheart. This will just be something to…help."

I didn't say anything else when Daddy and Grandma Jen and I all piled back into the car. Daddy asked to be dropped off at the coffee shop three blocks from home so he could do his work there, and he ran into the shop as rain fell onto his back.

When Grandma Jen and I pulled into the driveway, I almost didn't want to get out of the car. I didn't know how to feel. Medication sounds like such a scary word. I'm not sick.

I'm not.

Mommy was making herself a green smoothie at the counter and had her back to us when Grandma Jen and I walked in. I tried the smoothie last week and gagged. Clover from Mommy's Facebook group says the smoothie is the equivalent of seven years at the doctor, whatever that means. Mommy turned to look over her shoulder and saw Grandma Jen and me.

"Is school out early?" she asked. "I don't think school is out early. What are you doing, Jen?"

I looked up at Grandma Jen, who was slowly removing her coat and then tying her gray hair in a loose bun.

"The better question, Karen, is what are you doing?" Grandma Jen motioned to the smoothie in process. "Is that what you're having for lunch? There's nothing in that for you, let alone the baby."

Mommy looked a little bit upset. "You know, the funny thing about science is that we learn more about it every day. It turns out that vegetables and leafy greens are super healthy and great for children. Who would have thought it? I'm drinking this before I do another baby soothing."

Grandma Jen shook her head. "The only baby that needs soothing is your current daughter. Did you even remember that today Cameron and I had a meeting with her teacher?" Mommy opened her mouth to say something, but Grandma Jen cut her off. "No, of course, you didn't because you're busy making a smoothie to deal with insignificant, irrelevant, and altogether improbable negative energy. Never mind how you were just a few months ago when my son dared to miss the same thing you just did. You should know, the school wants us to consider medication."

Mommy had started ignoring Grandma Jen after she was cut off, and she kept making her smoothie. "Are you done?

The baby is due in two days. You couldn't wait to say this? Arguing is bad for the baby. And medication is off the table. There is nothing wrong with my daughter."

Grandma Jen put her hands on her hips. Mommy's words actually made me feel better.

I said, "See, I'm fine, Grandma. Really. I don't need medication."

Grandma Jen waved me off. "You are amazing, but this is not okay. Karen, you can't wait two days to be a mother. You are a mother today, and you've been a mother these past three months while you've been dealing with your energy—"

"I can't take this right now, Jen, I really just—"

"Could you listen to me for just once in your life! Just once!" Grandma Jen screamed.

Mommy looked up from her smoothie, shocked. I was shocked too. I think I might have flinched, actually. It was scary. We don't scream in this family. We talk to each other in small insults using hushed tones when we're angry. Sometimes we yell. We never scream.

It scared me so much, and Mommy and Grandma Jen looked so angry, that I decided I couldn't stay in the house with them. I said, "I'm going to the backyard," and I didn't wait for a response.

I had my rain jacket on but no shoes, and I went out the glass sliding door in our living room and sat on our little patio. The clouds were hiding the sun, and the shadows of trees seemed long and like they were claws coming to tear me apart.

I didn't put up my hood. The water beat down on my head and dripped onto my nose and rolled down my cheeks.

I breathed out, finally, when I was sitting on that patio. I could hear that Mommy and Grandma Jen were still fighting, but the tone got quieter and less angry. I wondered if maybe you were crying, and that was why it was raining. Whenever Grandma Jen and Mommy fight, I want to cry.

When I got too cold, I went back inside.

I heard Grandma Jen say, from the kitchen still, "You're not alone, Karen. We *will* get through this together."

I made my way into the kitchen, making splish-splash noises the whole way there.

Mommy was sitting on the floor with her head resting on her knees and her back to the counter. She was crying. "How come you're the one who always believes you know what to do? How come you're the one who gets to get it right? I'm her mother, Jennifer, so why is it that I can't even understand her? I'm her *mother.*"

I didn't know what to do. Mommy looked as broken on the outside as I felt on the inside. I stayed on the edge of the kitchen and hugged myself a bit. "You don't get everything wrong, Mommy. And Grandma Jen doesn't get everything right."

Mommy looked up from her knees and stared at me. "You're wet." After a long pause, she said in an almost childish tone, "Grandma Jen doesn't get everything right?"

I nodded. "Remember that time she went onto the north highway instead of the south one, and we almost ended up in Canada instead of Florida?"

Mommy gave me a weak laugh. "Yeah, if I hadn't caught it, we'd have been at the border." I looked up and saw Grandma Jen pouring out the green smoothie and then all of the kale juice.

Mommy noticed when Grandma Jen began pouring out the almond milk.

"What are you doing?" Mommy yelled. "I need that!"

Grandma Jen shrugged. "I was taking advantage of your sanity. Aren't we moving past this habit of yours?"

What Mommy said next was too inappropriate, but I learned the F word.

That word was so dirty, I went back outside and allowed the rain to wash that feeling of ickiness away. Mommy and Grandma Jen started fighting again. I could hear yells through the glass.

Maybe they'll make up soon. Maybe there will be a rainbow tomorrow.

Do you think you could make one?

I don't like the rain.

I hope you're not crying,

Miss W

PS

I don't like that I'm not allowed to eat sugar, but according to the healthy plate diagram in Mr. Odber's room, Mommy does a better job of eating the right foods than Grandma Jen. Grandma Jen's destruction of the smoothie things might be another thing she got wrong.

Dear the Man Upstairs,

After Mommy and Grandma Jen's fight, Mommy agreed to let Grandma Jen take me to Dr. Keaty and discuss medication options. "I'm not saying yes. I want to be clear about that. I just want us to get some information. I still think it might not be a good idea."

Grandma Jen had nodded and said, "That's nice dear." We went to Dr. Keaty right after.

When Grandma Jen came in instead of Mommy, Dr. Keaty raised an eyebrow but didn't say anything. When we were partway through explaining all my struggles at school,

Grandma Jen asked, "What might medication look like for Miss W?"

Dr. Keaty looked kinda worried. "I understand that Karen is on bedrest, which is why you are here, but are you sure that she is she okay with this line of questioning? We've discussed medication before, and she has never supported it. Does she know you're asking about this?"

I said, "Yes, Mommy knows. She just wants information."

Dr. Keaty relaxed. "Well, in that case, I'll send you home with a pamphlet. Your medication will target hyperactivity and help you focus. We could either give it to you in the form of pills or a powder to be mixed in with your food."

I shrugged. "I like powder." This is true; I do like powder. Powder looks kind of like snow, and it smells like nothing, so I feel like I'm an alien whenever I see it.

Dr. Keaty nodded seriously to Grandma Jen. "We'd give her a controlled dose in powder then. We can do a trial run for about a month and then adjust based on her response."

Grandma Jen pursed her lips. "And it would help?"

Dr Keaty gave Grandma Jen a gentle smile. "Miss W is already high functioning, and it is my firm belief based on all our sessions that she has immense capacity for growth. I don't want you to think of the medications as 'help' so much as an aid to allow her to achieve her maximum potential." Dr Keaty passed Grandma Jen a form and a pamphlet with a picture of six kids smiling on the front with a swing set behind them. "All the information Karen and Cameron need is in there. As soon as both of her parents sign the form I gave you, I can fill the prescription."

"Well, then, this has been very informative." Grandma Jen went out into the office, and I got to talk to Dr Keaty alone.

Dr. Keaty was wearing a blue sweater, and she looked so pretty when the light from the window hit her chocolate-colored skin. "How do you feel about getting medicated?"

"I don't know." I picked at a little bit of lint on the couch. "I don't think I'm sick."

"You are not sick," Dr. Keaty said. "I don't want you to ever think that. Sometimes, Miss W, people are born with a sandbag attached to their ankle. Some of those people never learn how to walk. Some of those people not only learn how to walk, but then they also learn how to run. Medication will be a way to free you from your sandbag."

"But if I can run," I asked, "why would I need to let go of my sandbag?"

Dr. Keaty leaned forward. "Because," she said in a hushed whisper, "those people who learn how to run with their sandbags, people like you, can do amazing things when they are freed from them. Without extra weight attached to their ankles, they can learn to *fly*."

That made me think of all the ways it feels like I'm weighed down during the day. I feel like it is so hard for me to do things sometimes, like finish spelling tests.

"Would medication really help me focus?" I asked in a small voice.

"It should," Dr. Keaty promised. "And if it doesn't, we can always stop. You know, your mom has been having a hard time for a while, I think. Her considering medication is a sign that maybe she's letting go of her own sandbag."

"I hope so," I said.

Dr. Keaty looked at me with the kind of expression Grandma Jen gives me when she says she loves me. "I want you to know that I'm proud of you, Miss W. I really am."

That made me feel like the sun decided to use my chest as its new home, and I think I blushed. I don't know if I managed to say anything back to Dr. Keaty. I think I was too busy glowing.

When we were driving home, Grandma Jen said, "Well, your mother managed to do something right."

I said, "What?"

Grandma Jen said, "She found you a good doctor."

I disagreed. "Dr. Keaty isn't just a *good* doctor. She's the best."

Glowing,

Miss W

Dear the Man Upstairs,

Mommy and Daddy spent two days attempting to argue about whether to get me a prescription for medication. I kind of wanted Mommy to win. Nina and Momo are my best friends, and they don't need any medication or pills or powder to make them act like super awesome normal fifth graders. Even Stupid Sean Hanner doesn't need to take anything to act like a regular kid at school.

It just feels like something else that makes me different, and I have enough of those. No one else has red hair, or green eyes, or a Dr. Keaty, or even a grandpa who died when their dad was fifteen. Sometimes I feel like Momo and I are the only two girls who really understand what it's like to be different because Momo is the only Japanese American girl in the whole school. But she has a whole family in Milwaukee. Mommy and Daddy say I'm nothing like them.

When they were fighting, Daddy would say, "If the meds will get the school off our back, what do you have to lose?"

Mommy would yell, "It's not about me, Cameron. It's about *our* daughter. It's about what *we* have to lose," and then she'd get quiet and say, "I can't do this right now. The baby is due any minute."

Daddy would say, "This can't wait. We have a daughter right now."

Mommy would respond, "You sound like your mother."

"Well, maybe she's onto something, huh?"

"I can't believe I let you talk me into living with Jen."

"Do you really think you could do any of this without her here?"

"She's not here right now, is she?"

This is true. Grandma Jen has started going on even more walks all dressed up. Last night, I saw her come back to the door with an old man who looks like the same man I saw walking a dog when we first toured the new house we now live in. I saw it all from my bedroom window.

This new house has stairs, which is where I sit to listen to Mommy and Daddy argue about me. I don't like hearing them argue. It makes me think that they're going to leave each other, like how Yvette Guiteau's parents got divorced. That happened when we were in second grade, and I think sometimes maybe that's why she's so mean. I don't want to be mean, but sometimes when I worry about Mommy and Daddy fighting, I feel angry.

When Mommy and Daddy were fighting, I spent the days throwing Mr. Wiggles into the walls and then apologizing to him. He's just a stuffed bear, though, so he can't get mad at me or really tell me anything to make this better.

I guess Daddy won the argument. He and I went to Dr. Keaty and got the prescription filled, and it was also the first time he and Dr. Keaty met in person.

I got to talk with Dr. Keaty more about the fifth-grade checklist. This last session we worked on attention, and she helped guide me through a couple of really boring worksheets with breathing and muscle-tensing techniques.

This morning was the first time I had medication powder—which I've decided to call the snow of death—in my yogurt before school.

Ms. Langies ignored me when she saw me come into the classroom after ducking under the still-fallen daisy chain, but I just stuck my tongue at her from behind my hand. I was pretending to yawn.

We were working on stories today. I kept waiting for the feeling I get when I know I just have to move. I kept waiting for my mind to go somewhere else and not come back. I did feel a need to swing my legs, so I swung them. Rainbow light reflecting off Ms. Genever's watch did distract me. But I was able to finish my short story without getting up except one time to go to the bathroom, and no one in the class could believe it. I walked to the music classroom and back without skipping once. (I wanted to skip, but then I thought that maybe then I would make people think the medication wasn't working, and I don't want people to think that.)

Sean Hanner came over and asked me if I was okay because I was acting so weird. I told him that I'm doing fine, and he said to talk to him if something is really hard. I just laughed and said that I was too close to being at my maximum potential to find anything hard. Then he flicked my forehead and said, "Yeah, right. You're about as advanced as my pencil."

So then I licked his hand and said, "I feel bad for your pencil."

Stupid Sean Hanner wiped his hand on his jeans. "If you can relate to my pencil, you're probably not so different from it."

I looked at him, shocked, before I decided that was funny. We both laughed, and he went back to sit at his desk.

At recess, Momo was braiding my hair, and I was feeding her pretzels like she was a baby bird. Nina was giving Alex moon eyes.

Momo said, "Sean likes you."

I shrugged. "I don't think so."

Momo turned to Nina. "She's blind," she exclaimed dramatically. "Back me up here, Nina. She's so blind it's a concern. She's oblivious."

Nina calmly ate a couple of grapes. "It's a talent," she agreed. She hadn't stopped looking at Alex.

When we got into line order to go back upstairs when lunch was over, Momo kept poking me in my shoulder (she stands behind me) and saying, "I bet you ten dollars that if you ask him out, he'll say yes."

I whisper-yelled, "He would not!"

Ms. Langies noticed, and she said to me, "Ms. W, how dare you distract another student?"

But we weren't even in the classroom yet, and Momo was the one who talked, so I said, "I'm sorry, Ms. Langies. I didn't think I was distracting anybody."

Ms. Langies said, "That's your problem. You never *think*."

I felt a little bit like crying, and I couldn't say anything because my lip was wobbling so bad.

Needless to say, I was sent to the vice principal, but this time, I got a lollipop. I was confused because this is my second office visit of the year, and I thought that this would be a big deal and parents would be called and the whole shebang. Vice Principal Viceport said that after contacting specialists and reviewing my academic file, they've decided that special ed won't be a good fit and that Ms. Langies and I also seem to not be a good fit.

He said that he and the guidance counselor have decided to move me into Mr. Odber's class for a probationary period and that he wants to see if I can perform up to fifth-grade standards with a different teacher.

I said, "I won't let you down, Mr. Viceport."

He looked at me over the shiny wooden desk with very serious eyes. "I'll give you the benefit of the doubt." And that seemed really good, so I no longer felt like crying. In fact, I felt like doing maybe about a million jumping jacks, but I didn't, because I didn't want Vice Principal Viceport to change his mind about letting me change classes and not go to special ed.

I spent the afternoon with Nina in Mr. Odber's class, which was super fun, and he was very good-natured about me joining in. I was still tired and not normal energetic because of the snow of death I'd had in my yogurt during the morning.

Surprisingly, it was Nina's mom who picked me up at the end of the day.

"Where's Grandma Jen?" I was so excited to tell everyone I moved classes.

Yerena, Nina's mom, said, "With your mom, who is having a baby."

I yelled, "What? When? Where? How? Is she okay? Is the baby okay? Did she lose the baby? She didn't, right?"

Yerena said, "She's fine. Everything is fine."

"Promise?" I asked.

"I promise."

Nina tried to distract me when we got to her house, but I couldn't stop thinking about babies and deliveries and dead little brothers and going to heaven early.

When we were eating a snack, Yerena's phone rang. She talked for a few minutes and announced, "The delivery went smoothly. Both your mom and your sister are alive and well. You'll stay here tonight, and tomorrow your mom will come home from the hospital, and you'll get to meet baby Elizabeth."

"Anthophila," I corrected. I felt so relieved. Mommy and my sister were fine.

"What?" Yerena asked.

"Her name is not Elizabeth. It's Anthophila. An for short. That's what I'm going to call her."

Yerena looked confused. "Anthophila is not her name."

"But it is a better name than Elizabeth. People should always do what's best, Mommy says."

Sincerely,

A Big Sister

Dear Miss W, A Big Sister,

Congratulations on the birth of your baby sister! New lives are always something to celebrate. I remember when your mother was born. She weighed just seven pounds and four ounces. Do you know how much your little sister weighed when she was born?

I think this next year will be a little hard for you, but it will be filled with hard things and wonderful things. Babies are a lot of work, and they cry often. As a big sister, you will sometimes need to calm your sister down. She will be loud in the nighttime, and that means it's important you sleep whenever you can. If you need help, reach out. Once again, congratulations on this happy occasion. I'll miss the days of hearing about baby Anthophila in your mother's stomach, but I'm excited to hear about all the adventures the two of you will share.

Fondly,

the Man Upstairs

PART III

PUPA

Dear the Man Upstairs,

Mommy wasn't allowed to come home from the hospital until she was ready, and she took thirty-six hours. My baby sister weighed seven pounds and one ounce when she was born. I weighed six pounds and three ounces when I was born, so maybe my baby sister is going to be taller than me when she finishes growing up. Because Mommy was in the hospital, I spent the night with Nina, and I went to school in the morning with her, and I went to class with her because I am now in her class with Mr. Odber.

I came in with her, and he announced, "Our red-haired addition will be joining us for a few weeks."

I smiled and waved, but I felt a little weird. Everyone already kind of knew me, though, so it all worked out. Mr. Odber told me to tell everyone my name, so I did, and they all laughed because they had learned it a month ago when I started getting kicked out of Ms. Langies's room all the time and also most of them have known me since kindergarten, anyway.

I met with Mr. Batra during lunch because he is the man in charge of class assignments, and he told me that I would be in the room with Mr. Odber until winter break (which is in two and half months) and then I would be moved back into my old class. I said that Ms. Langies and I were just not a good fit, because that's what Mr. Viceport told me, and then I said that it wasn't her, it was me. Mr. Batra laughed and said that it very well may have been her, and that in the spring semester, there would be a whole new teacher in the class.

This got me very excited. I asked if Mrs. N would be our new teacher and he said no, that Mrs. N was going to keep teaching in the fourth grade as she had for the past fifteen years. I sighed and decided to move on with my life, so I told him that later that night, I was going to meet my sister for the very first time, which made him say, "Aww. Isn't that precious?"

He said it in a kind of cooing sort of voice, like the sounds Mommy makes to baby Anthophila when she's doing a baby-soothing. This made me decide that I did not like Mr. Batra. I'm not the baby in the family. When I went back outside, there were four minutes left for lunch and Stupid Sean Hanner came over. He wanted to know where I had been, so I told him about moving classes, and then he said that class wasn't as fun without me. So I said that class wasn't as good without him either, but I would be coming back after winter break, which is way far in the future. Then Sean Hanner said that maybe we could have playdates or sit together at lunches sometimes, and I said I wasn't ready to commit, but our families were having a picnic in about a month. So then the bell rang.

Sean began to go to Ms. Langies's line, but he turned around and said, "You're really cool for a girl."

I thought about how I was cool and how he had been super cool in standing up for me. So I said to him, "You're the coolest boy I know, even though you are pretty stupid."

He grinned. "Am not."

I stuck out my tongue. "Are too, but only sometimes."

And then he had to be quiet because Ms. Langies was watching but he did the hand motions to show that if he was stupid, so was I. And I didn't want to disagree with that one because for some reason the idea of being like Sean Hanner didn't bother me so much. That is, until Momo made eye contact with me and drew a heart in the air and made a kissing face. Then I glared at her until she started giggling, and I knew that just like Nina, Momo and I were going to be friends forever. Yvette glared at me and giggled about something with Samantha Adams, but Yvette and I are never going to be friends. So I told myself I didn't care and pretended that I didn't feel like my stomach was dropping out of my feet.

Grandma Jen picked me up from school, and I realized that Gammy and Gampa (my mommy's parents) had arrived in time for the birth, so they were sitting in our living room on the brand-new blue couch. Gammy made me mac and cheese, which was exactly cheesy enough. I gave all three grandparents a dance recital and they clapped and told me I was the best in the world. I knew that they were just saying that to be nice, but that didn't make it any less fun to hear.

Then Mommy came home holding a little, green-blanketed bundle in her arms and leaning heavily on Daddy, and I just ran right over. I looked underneath the blankets, called a swaddle I have now learned, and saw my sister. She had blue eyes, but Daddy says they probably won't be blue forever, and this little tuft of red hair like Mommy and me, and the cutest face anyone has ever had, maybe even cuter than the face I had when I was little.

"Can I hold her?" I asked.

Daddy showed me how to support the baby's head and Mommy handed Elizabeth to my arms.

Mommy said, "That's your sister. You're a big sister."

I was looking at her big (but still little) eyes, and her tiny little lips, and her super wrinkly face, and her kind of squished nose, and although I thought it should have been super ugly, it somehow looked adorable. I thought she was going to be an ugly duckling like me, but I think she's going to look like a swan from day one. "Hello, Ellie-An, it's me, your big sister."

She smiled in her sleep and even though I had to hand her away to Gampa because she was heavy, I had decided that I loved her and would protect her. It is my biggest most important job.

"Ellie-An?" Daddy pulled me into a hug as he said this, and I squeezed back.

"Ellie, short for Elizabeth, and An short for Anthophila."

Gampa was holding Ellie-An and kind of swaying back and forth.

"Ellie-An," Gampa said. "It's a good nickname." He brought Ellie-An closer to his face. "Well, hello there, my dear. I see that you have great things in your future, just like your big sister."

Mommy patted my head. "Ellie-An," she said. "Well, I don't hate it."

Gampa passed the baby to Grandma Jen. She said, "Ellie-An it is."

Sincerely,

Ellie-An's Big and Only Sister

Dear the Man Upstairs,

The stupid baby hasn't stopped crying. All night for these whole two weeks, she's been super loud, and I wasn't able to sleep at all. I threw a pillow at the wall last night because of how *loud* everything was. I was so tired, and the baby was crying and *crying and crying,* and I just wanted to *sleep.* But I didn't. Sleep. I haven't slept in like three days. I think I might be going crazy. I normally wouldn't have had problems in school because I always seem to gain energy the less

I sleep, but with the new medications, I've started falling into dreamland during class.

I hate it.

I feel like I'm not myself. It was an important piece of me that I could always have energy no matter where I was, even if it was midnight on an airplane and Mommy and Daddy just wanted me to be asleep. That was who I was. And now I have to take this stupid powder in my yogurt every morning, and I feel like I'm someone else. I feel like I'm a tiger who lost my legs, just sort of crawling through life on my stomach and missing the days when I used to be able to run.

I asked Mommy and Daddy for help, but they said, "That's part of being a big sister to a newborn. You cried, too, when you were this young."

Grandma Jen's been going to the doctor a lot. She's also been going on a lot of walks with lipstick on. I did manage to tell her that I've been feeling really tired recently, so she said she's gonna try and help as best as she can. That was yesterday already, and she hasn't fixed it yet. I can't keep living like this. I really can't.

Mr. Odber doesn't really notice I'm falling asleep more often because most fifth graders are always kinda sorta falling asleep, but Coach Summers has definitely noticed. (I've been on his swim team this year instead of dancing because it turns out little girls can't become bees no matter how much dance practice they do. Also, who wants to live for just four years? Not me. I have things to do, places to be, people to see.)

A few practices ago, Coach Summers told me to "pick up the pace" and this last practice he pulled me out of the pool and told me that I was "too fatigued" and needed to "rest good and long." In one month, I'll be competing for the first time with my team, so I guess he really wants me to be in the best shape I can be.

My new friend Mon from swim team told me after practice that, "I missed you in the pool. Get better soon."

Because Ellie-An has been making so much noise, I've been having a really hard time sleeping. Yesterday I felt really sick to my stomach all day. I didn't eat very much for dinner because it just seemed kinda gross. Gampa asked me what was wrong.

Daddy said, "What doesn't kill you makes you stronger," and Grandma Jen was out of the house but Gammy was there.

She said, "That's a load of BS if I ever heard it, Cameron. Are you feeling alright, sweetheart?"

I let out a kind of low groaning sound and then Gampa said, nodding his head, "She's sick as a dog, this one."

Mommy's face went all pale like *she* was the sick one, and she bundled Ellie-An right up and said, "I can't be around someone who's sick. I have a newborn!"

Gammy helped Mommy go to a room without me and calm down while Gampa got the thermometer out and put it under my tongue. He glared at Daddy the whole time, as if me being sick was somehow Daddy's fault. I don't think Gampa likes Daddy very much, but maybe I'm reading too much into his actions. I just remember one time when I was four years old, I ran out into the street and Gampa ran after me and afterward he said something to Daddy that sounded suspiciously like, "I don't know what my daughter sees in you. She could do so much better." But childhood memories aren't perfect facts, so I could have imagined the whole thing. Life is full of mysteries.

The thermometer informed us that I did in fact have a fever, and then I threw up dinner, and well…Gampa made Daddy clean that mess up. Daddy didn't really want to, but

Gampa said, "What doesn't kill you makes you stronger. Isn't that right, Cameron?"

So then I changed into my pajamas, and Grandma Jen came home, and she helped me brush my teeth and tucked me in for bed. I thought it was very nice that Grandma Jen was so helpful with my illness because she's been leaving the house a lot these days. Ever since Ellie-An came into my life two weeks ago, Grandma Jen's been going on outings and getting dressed up, and I don't know why. Even so, she made time for me when I needed her.

Because I was sick (and am still, just a little), I was not allowed to be around Mommy or Ellie-An. Mommy's been sending me little messages. Daddy will hand me Post-it notes at breakfast that say "I love you/good morning" or I'll get a picture of Mommy with Ellie-An. Every now and again, I get notes that say, "Clean up your room or I'll know," which feels a little bit threatening, but Mommy will be Mommy.

Sincerely,
A Girl with the Flu

Dear the Man Upstairs,

It took me about three full days to be healthy enough to go back to school and swim team, and Mommy decided it would be another week before she would let me see her and Ellie-An, but I'm all good now.

My life has become mysterious. I think Grandma Jen is either training for a marathon or keeping a secret. Grandma Jen is going on "walks" every day all the time now, and sometimes for more than two hours. She was super weird and suspicious just last night, like why would she go on a walk at dinnertime for two hours while wearing her favorite scarf and lipstick? It seemed weird to me.

My theory is that she is interviewing for teaching jobs, but Daddy has a different theory. He said that he thinks Grandma Jen is "seeing someone." I told him of course she was. She sees lots of people every day. Like she sees me, Daddy, Mommy, and Ellie-An for starters. But Daddy said that "seeing someone" means dating someone, and I said that was a perfectly ridiculous saying, because just because Grandma Jen sees me, it doesn't mean we're dating.

Daddy said, "Never mind. You'll understand when you're older," which is mugwump because I never understand anything, and I keep getting older.

Anyways, Mr. Bennet, the man with the dog I saw when we first saw the house, dropped Grandma Jen off that night, so Daddy and I guess that maybe he is dating Grandma Jen. I don't know if he's good enough for her, though, so I am going to see him soon to investigate.

Next week, I don't have to take my medications at all on Saturday and Sunday so I can be super energetic for the swim meet. I'm really looking forward to that. I can just be myself for a full two days. The meds aren't perfect, either. Mr. Odber has definitely gotten annoyed with me a couple times because I really can't finish spelling tests all the time without getting a little distracted or at least swinging my legs.

Grandma Jen got worried when I told her that Mr. Odber seemed a little bit annoyed with me once after a spelling test, and she emailed him and he sent her an email back saying something like, *Fifth grade is just right for Miss W. She's behaving age-appropriately, which means she sometimes has a hard time focusing.*

That made me feel a little bit better. It's good to know that I'm not so different from the other kids. Grandma Jen said, "Mr. Odber seems like a good teacher." I think he is, but he's also really old so I'm not sure how much longer he'll keep teaching.

Oh, but I got off topic! I was telling you about the swim meet. Mommy is super excited about the whole thing. She told me that if I win anything, she'll buy me a Snickers bar and that I should stay a swimmer forever. She said something about, "This will get you into college"

Daddy said, "Don't say something prematurely, Karen."

I remember learning all about babies, and I said, "No, I was born on time and so was Ellie-An." As soon as I said that, Ellie-An started crying, and Mommy had to go upstairs with the baby. Ellie-An is cute, but all she does is eat and cry. I love her, but I don't know that I *like* her. I can't wait for her to grow up.

Speaking of growing up, Sean Hanner (who might be less stupid than Yvette Guiteau who keeps tripping me during recess and calling me a baby for reasons that are clearly mean) had his birthday this week. I got him a bag of really good caramel corn and the teddy bear to pay him back for the cookies he got me for my birthday last year.

I'm not in Ms. Langies class anymore so I had to go find him during lunch break. I told Nina what I was going to do when Momo was in the bathroom because I didn't want her saying I was in love or anything. I'm not. I don't even like Stupid Sean Hanner. He's a boy. So. Ew.

But even though I don't like him, he's been nice to me this year.

I went over to where he was hanging out with his friends Nathan, Alex, and Pierce by the picnic tables, and I kinda just pushed the gifts at him. I was on my way to running away but then he called out, "Hey, Miss W."

I turned around and waited for a second.

"Thanks," he said.

I blinked. "You're welcome."

Sean smiled at me and ran a hand through his sand-colored hair. "No, really, thank you."

I nodded and went back. Alex punched Sean in the arm. Boys can be so violent. When I went back to my friends, I saw that Momo had returned from the bathroom.

"How wonderful it must be to be in love," she cried. I punched her in the arm. She said, "Ow," which was much better than all that love moosh.

Sincerely,

Miss W, a Girl Who Is NOT in Love

Dear the Man Upstairs,

The day after Sean's birthday, Gammy and Gampa had to go back to Nashville because they don't actually live in Milwaukee. I think they should move here. I told them they should move, but they were like, "We have lives outside of you," which I thought was really unfair. Everyone has lives; it's just that their lives would be *better* if they lived with us full time, like Grandma Jen. I'm really glad she lives with us now instead of us living in an apartment a full twenty minutes away from her studio. She makes me breakfast sometimes when Mommy can't because of taking care of Ellie-An.

Grandma Jen has still been going out all the time with Mr. Bennet and sometimes on her own. Grandma Jen brought me to a doctor's appointment with a regular doctor (not Dr. Keaty) for my flu shot (which I should have gotten earlier this year, but Mommy's been baby-crazy these last few months) because she said, "It was no trouble." It was no trouble, it turned out, because she had a doctor's appointment herself.

Maybe Mr. Bennet is a doctor, and she went on a date? It's hard to know everything about my family. I'm just one person.

Speaking of doctors, Dr. Keaty thinks that swim team is a great place for me to get out energy. Coach Summers would agree with her. He says that I have "real potential to go pro," which is a "long shot at best, but still on the table." Sometimes Coach Summers reminds me of my dad.

Everything is a long shot to Ellie-An. She can't even hold her head up all the way. She just cries and poops, and then I have to change her diaper whenever Mommy just can't do it anymore.

I spend many afternoons rubbing cream all over Ellie-An's little body, and she just snuffles and says nothing. Sometimes I talk to her and say things like, "You are a baby. One day, when you're older, you'll be so embarrassed when I tell you I changed your diapers."

Her embarrassment will be fun to see because I really hate changing her diapers. They smell weird, and I need to wash my hands for a full twenty seconds after. Sometimes Ellie-An cries when I'm changing her diaper, which feels really unfair because I'm the one who wants to cry from how loud she is.

Because Ellie-An cries all the time, I'm really happy to be able to go to swim practice a lot. Even though I'm a fifth grader, I get to practice with the middle school swim team twice a week.

I like diving into the water early in the morning and kicking my legs as hard as they will go so that I can work off some energy. Every time I swim, it reminds of when I used to dance. I feel like I'm flying.

I made a friend too. His name is Monty, but everyone calls him Mon. He is always tired on Mondays. So we always tell him on Mondays, "You can do it!" On Fridays, he swims so fast, he sets records. He's the only kid my age on the team. The team is mostly seventh and eighth graders, and there are a few sixth graders. Mon and I are the only fifth graders. (I like having someone my age because some of the seventh graders complain that we're too little to be in the pool with them and can get kind of aggressive.)

Mon is the best. I got into the pool one morning, and I was about to warm up with some laps.

Mon just rushed up to me and he was all like, "Do you want to hear a joke?"

I said, "Yes."

He said, "Knock knock."

I replied, "Who's there?"

He said, "Interrupting cow."

I started to say, "Interrupting cow wh—" but he cut me off and yelled "MOO!"

"Oh," I said, "I get it! You interrupted me because you're the interrupting cow."

Mon gave me a kind of bow and splashed some water in my face. I laughed at him. He joined in, and we were both giggling.

The rest of the day, we would moo at the eighth graders, but then we accidentally moo-ed at Coach Summers when he told us to swim more laps and he shook his head.

"This is a moo-free zone," he told us.

Coach Summers made us promise we would never moo at him again, but I just have a feeling the "interrupting cow" will be back.

This coming weekend is my first-ever swim meet, and Coach Summers thinks I'll win. Coach Summers laughed in surprise when I broke my own record swimming one time when Grandma Jen picked me up from practice. He said to her (about me), "This girl is made for cardio."

Grandma Jen winked and said, "Darn straight. This girl was made to move."

I covered my ears and whispered, "Grandma Jen don't use the d-word. It's bad for my development." I'm a smart girl, and I know the d-word, the c-word, and the s-word (stupid), are all not to be said in public. The only acceptable curse word according to Mommy is the sh-word, (not to be repeated here) which can only be yelled when drivers are bad on the roads, and it is absolutely not allowed—no sir, no ma'am—under her roof.

After I said that, Grandma Jen just lost it and so did Coach Summers and they were just hooting and then Grandma Jen was all like, "Oh, sorry, I didn't mean to jeopardize your development."

Coach Summers chuckled, "Oh, ma'am, she's got you there."

Grandma Jen was still smiling the whole drive home and shaking her head. I don't know why my telling the truth was so funny, but I guess anything that makes Grandma Jen laugh that much can't be all bad.

Grandma Jen told Mommy about what I said, and Mommy laughed a bunch, too, and then Daddy came in to find out what all the fuss was about, and then he was laughing, so they were all three laughing. When enough people are laughing, I have to laugh, too, so then I started laughing, and then Ellie-An was laughing with high-pitched giggles and big breaths in between. That was so funny a noise we all just started laughing again.

I got the hiccups and so did Mommy, so we had to drink a whole glass of water with our nose plugged. At the end of that, we sat together on the couch, my head in her lap, and she whispered in my ear, "I'm so proud of you, my love." I guess she really wanted me to stand up for no swearing. It might be the first time she's said she's proud of me since I was really little.

Warmly,

Miss W, A Swimmer

Dear the Man Upstairs,

This weekend was finally my first-ever swim meet, and I made Mommy proud again. It's February, it is snowing outside, there is ice on the roads, and my swim meet is just keeping on keeping on because it's indoors at the YMCA, anyways.

Me and Mon were Coach Summer's youngest competitors. He told us poolside before the competition, "You two are the only fifth graders on this team because you are the only two worth training for real and not for babysitting."

Mon got all up and puffy and said, "You know it, Coach." He can be very proud of himself when he's got his eye on the prize.

I said, "I'm worth babysitting, too, Coach. Amy really liked me."

Coach Summers gave me this fond smile and ruffled my hair, but nothing happened because it was all tucked up in a swim cap. "I bet she did, but babysitting ain't my passion."

This made sense to me, and I said, "I get it. Science is not my passion, but some people really like it. I didn't mean to say that you and Amy need to be exactly the same." Dr. Keaty has been telling me how important it is to tell the adults in my life that they don't all have to be exactly like Grandma Jen or Mrs. N or other ideas in my head, and that I need to tell them that it's okay for them to be their own people.

Coach tried to hold in a chuckle but couldn't, so he laughed once. He got serious and said, "That's very understanding of you."

I nodded solemnly; it is my goal in life to be understanding and kind.

The meet had this "ladies first" rule, so I went in for the two-hundred-meter freestyle and one-hundred-meter butterfly. For the freestyle, I jumped in as soon as the fake gun that shoots smoke went up, and I just was flying. I remember feeling this sense of peace when I was under the water. I broke a record or something, and I won that race, and butterfly too. Mon came in second in both his races, and then a seventh grader named Steve's freestyle two-hundred-meter was slower than mine by a full second. That's funny because he's older, taller, and a boy, which apparently means he's supposed to be better than me.

Coach was really proud of all of his swimmers, he said, but I could tell that he was proudest of me, and he was telling anyone who would listen that I was his student.

Grandma Jen hugged me as soon as soon as the meet was officially over, even though I hadn't changed and was still wet.

Ellie-An tried to grab me, but Daddy held her back because wet babies are too much work. But then Mommy, who had given Ellie-An to Daddy, came over, made a face, and then she hugged me too. Her fuzzy boots got wet, which I know makes her unhappy, but as soon as she decided to hug me, she hugged me tight. She stepped away when she was done and stole my towel so she could dry herself off.

She looked suspiciously happy even though she was wet. "You just got all the athleticism in the family, didn't you? I couldn't be prouder of you for this."

That was the second time in two days Mommy said she was proud of me. I'd just won, and I had all these emotions running around, and I guess I couldn't take them all at the same time, so I started crying.

"What's wrong, champ?" Daddy asked.

I looked up at them, trying to smile because the tears wouldn't stop. "Nothing's wrong," I said, and I believed it too.

I went home smiling like Grandma Jen had after practice, and Grandma Jen kept on looking at Mommy in the front seat and shaking her head, saying, "You need to tell her you're proud more often."

Mommy muttered, "You need to stay of out of my business."

Daddy and I played with Ellie-An, who was getting super into the song "The Itsy-Bitsy Spider."

That night, I had a hard time going to sleep, and I woke up to Daddy and Mommy arguing.

"It doesn't have to be Harvard," Mommy was saying. "We could get her a Yale sweatshirt."

"Come on, Karen, let's not give her that much pressure when she's so young."

"I don't mean it be pressure, Cam. It would be empowering. It would let her know that I believe in her."

"Then just tell her that."

"It might help her get motivated, you know, to—"

"Our daughter does not have to go to an Ivy for her swimming to have been worthwhile. We are not sending her that message."

"What about giving her something small, like a pamphlet? Just information."

"Karen."

"Alright, alright. I can wait until next year."

"Karen, no—"

Mommy let out a loud huff. "We'll come back to it."

They were silent for a while. After a bit, I heard Daddy say, "She's amazing. And we're doing our best, aren't we?"

"Well, you finally are. I can see that. I don't know what to do anymore, Cam. It's just I was so worried about losing Ellie-An, but now she's here, and I look back at this last year, and I think I did so many things wrong. Do you think I'm a good parent, Cam?"

Mommy sounded really sad when she said that and vulnerable.

"I don't know what to say, Karen. You always do what you think is best," Daddy replied.

Mommy sniffled. "Right. Yeah. Look at where that got me. I think maybe I should stop shooting for being the best and start shooting for alright."

I went up to bed and held Mr. Wiggles close to my heart. I feel like I get Mommy. I'm not always doing good, even with the new medications and everything. Mr. Odber has gotten a few headaches because I couldn't sit still, and even with my meds, I have a hard time focusing for a whole spelling test, and sometimes I don't finish. I don't think that I can always do good, but these days, just like Mommy, I'll start shooting for alright.

Sincerely.

Miss W

Dear the Man Upstairs,

Remember how Grandma Jen wore a scarf to my swim meet? Well, that was two weeks ago already (sorry for not writing sooner!), and now she's started wearing scarves around her head every day. She's gotten really into them. She has six so far, and my favorite is one that's blue, green, and purple, and it feels like she's wearing the Great Lake on her head.

She also has begun matching her lipstick to the scarves. She'll pair her red leaf scarf with red lipstick, and her ocean scarf with light pink. I think it's because she's trying to make Mr. Bennet fall even more in love with her. (I really need to meet him in person. I think he might be coming over for dinner soon.) If I were an old man and wasn't too busy thinking about how my back hurt, I would totally fall in love with Grandma Jen.

I don't think I would fall in love with Mommy though. She's gone crazy. Mommy has decided to go back into business. She decided that now that Ellie-An is a whole two months old, it's about time. She wants to work from home, and Daddy can help out with Ellie-An and me more these days because three out of five days a week, he stays home writing grants and proposals for his work. Grandma Jen helps out a bunch, too, when she isn't busy dating Mr. Bennet. Or going to the doctor. She spends a lot of time at the doctor's these days.

I think that Mommy is still too busy freaking out over her "most optimal diet for cognitive development of infants" to also start working, but she made up her mind and all I can do now is support her.

Mommy decided that she will go back to work as an interior decorator, but she will be like a blogger kind of, so she will have suggestions on some web page and then she'll like order people things from Amazon and then they'll do what she says. She's decided the first step in getting her career on the road is to decorate our house so that it looks picture perfect.

I came home from school today to find that the living room had nothing in it. Nothing at all. Mommy put our tan couch and three red comfy chairs and polished wooden tables out on the street. Apparently, she got a couple of high school boys to help her move them. I really hope you're not feeling too sad, Mr. Man Upstairs, because if it rains, they will be gross and then I won't ever be able to use them again.

I asked Daddy to *do* something because even the chairs in the kitchen are starting to disappear, and Daddy said that it's been so long since Mommy did anything for herself that he was saving his disagreements up for a better fight. What does that even mean?

I ate my after-school snack of Go-Gurt today sitting on the floor while Mommy looked at our refrigerator and said, "I think that this fridge with a few colored magnets, you know green leaf magnets, would look much better. Don't you think so, sweetie?"

I was about to say, "No, I do not, thank you," but then I realized that Mommy was using her stupid baby voice and that she had been talking to Ellie-An the whole time.

Ellie-An is on my side because she started crying. Then Mommy got all flustered and went and changed the baby's diaper, and I was left all alone, still on the floor, still eating my Go-Gurt.

If I had all the power in the world, the only thing I would do is make Go-Gurts stay frozen no matter what. What about you, Man Upstairs? What would you do with all the power in the world?

Curiously,
Miss W

Dear Miss W,

I do appreciate your letters so much, and I am sorry to hear that all your furniture is being removed. That's probably a hard change. Your grandfather, Claude, was someone who was always moving and had his mind in a million places at once. He would often change up the furniture in his house whenever he had to move but had nowhere to go.

I believe that every action has a reaction. Sometimes when you do something, a good thing happens. Sometimes a bad thing happens. With all the power in the world, I could do a lot of good and a lot of bad. I would have to be very careful.

I think I would not change much at all. Every action has consequences, and I don't know how the world would change if nobody got sick. Some people would want to get rid of all the bees in the world because they are afraid of being stung. To those people, bees are nothing but something scary. They don't see that bees form strong communities and help flowers grow. I don't think any single person will ever be able to understand why illness exists, but maybe somehow, it helps spring blossom. I like to think that.

How is being with Mr. Odber? Is school going well?

Sincerely,
the Man Upstairs

Dear the Man Upstairs,

I kinda get what you're saying, but not enough to summarize it in my own words and teach a peer in pair-share, so I can't say I've done the STAR technique (summarize, teach, add your own view, remember) for understanding what you read.

I brought your letter to Daddy who said to wait until middle school and then try reading it again. He was kinda surprised by your letter.

He was all like, "Wow, I guess your mystery man can write after all." His office used to be this little semicircle near the end of the hallway window, but Mommy has removed all of his things and is getting him a new desk and chair to make it more pretty.

I really miss the couch, and the old-old couch from our apartment that didn't make the move, (why is *everything* changing?) but Mommy sold all the furniture on Craig's List, and I guess Craig liked our things a bunch. I wanted Mommy to put things on Angie's List because Angie lives four doors down and would let me sit on her couch sometimes because she has cats and misses her grandchildren, but Mommy said that it had to be Craig. I don't like Craig very much.

Mommy has also been buying things from Craig's List because apparently he sometimes sells things really cheap and with the tags still on. I feel like maybe Mommy is caring a bit too much about the way our house is going to look and a bit too little about me and Ellie-An, but Ellie-An is proving to be super independent, and she'll just tummy time without crying while Mommy does a bunch of random things all over.

Daddy's getting a little annoyed and told Mommy that we need a couch and the TV back up because he missed a basketball game, but Mommy said that the season isn't officially even starting yet. Daddy said that he missed an episode of a good TV show, and Mommy said that she missed her career even more. I said that I missed Grandma Jen and then both of my parents realized that Grandma Jen wasn't home.

Mommy said, "Oh, she must be at a doctor's appointment."

Daddy gave Mommy a look and said, "Right, *Quincey's* a doctor."

Quincey is Mr. Bennet's first name, but I felt like Daddy was lying and trying to get Mommy to lie too. I don't care if Mr. Bennet's not a doctor, but I don't know why Daddy would lie about that.

Guess Grandma Jen is still going on a lot of dates, but normally she only goes out for dinner and during the school day. Weird, huh?

But you asked me about school, and I got way off topic. I do that a lot. Yvette isn't in Mr. Odber's class, but her friend Samantha Adams is, and Samantha is proving to be the kind of person I don't like being around. When Mr. Odber announced that he was going to have us all do presentations about different parts of the Revolutionary War, Samantha and I were assigned a group together with Renard and Pierce.

Samantha said, out loud, "Mr. Odber, can I please, please, be in a group without her? She's so hard to be around."

Mr. Odber said, "You get who you get, and you don't get upset," which wasn't exactly the response I was hoping for. So this whole project, Samantha's been making these noises like she's angry with the work I'm doing, which doesn't even make sense. I'm working just as hard as anyone. And when I was swinging my legs and reading about the battle of Bunker Hill, she yelled out, "Ow. You kicked me!"

But I knew I hadn't. So I said, "No I didn't."

And then Samantha started to cry, and Mr. Odber came over and asked what was wrong and Samantha said, "Miss W kicked me!"

Mr. Odber sighed. "I know you have a hard time sitting still and you've been getting better, but this kind of behavior won't be tolerated. I'm giving you a strike, and if you get two more, I'll have to send you back to Mr. Viceport."

I said, "But I really didn't do anything, Mr. Odber. I really didn't."

He looked at me. "I know you didn't mean to, but I just can't ignore this forever."

That hurt. I tried to pretend that I wasn't crying but it didn't work very well, so then I asked if I could please be excused to go to the bathroom. He said I could, and Samantha stuck her tongue out at me.

For the rest of the project, I've been sitting on the ground away from Samantha so she can't say I did anything to her because I'm too far away for it to be believable. Dr. Keaty helped me come up with the solution.

Nina and Momo have decided that they won't go to Samantha's birthday party to support me. I would have decided that, too, only I wasn't invited.

Grandma Jen was mad about that because it's school policy that if you invite more than half the girls in the grade, you have to invite all of them. She brought me out to ice cream even though it's getting cold outside, and she flipped the end of her yellow head scarf (it matches her umbrella) dramatically and said, "You keep on being your best self, and some day, people like Samantha will realize that they have nothing on you."

So I licked a bit of orange-chocolate ice cream off my cone and mumbled, "What if my best isn't good enough?"

And Grandma Jen gave me the tightest hug known to man and whispered, fiercely, "Your best is better than all of us."

Sincerely,
Someone Who Is Good Enough

Dear the Man Upstairs,

How's it been going? I haven't asked about you in a while but I'm doing it now. I guess sometimes I feel like you must always be the same because you never really talk about yourself, but maybe that isn't true. Everyone goes through a hard time sometimes.

Like me right now. I'm going through a bit of a hard time. My medication has been making me feel like I'm not myself. Dr. Keaty decided to up my dose of it, even on days when I have swim practice, so that I can focus better on the spelling tests with Mr. Odber.

I just feel so tired. Nina doesn't make me laugh as hard as she used to, and Momo isn't as fun to joke around with, and when I look in the mirror, I'm not pretty anymore. I don't know what's happening, but I feel so exhausted, and I never want to go to school anymore.

Samantha's been gossiping about me with Lillian Everton and Yvette Guiteau during recess. I heard them saying they don't want the retard in their project. I tried not to cry during recess, which before medication would have been super easy because I could have just distracted myself with one of the posters, but I couldn't distract myself as well and then I couldn't forget so then I cried on the play structure. That only made them call me a baby, too, and then it was even worse.

The teasing got bad enough Mr. Odber asked me what was wrong because I looked upset during quiet time before lunch. I knew that it was a bad thing to tattle on some girls in my class if I ever want them to like me, so then I just said nothing, but I think we both knew that I was lying.

And then you'll never guess, Stupid Sean Hanner came over one lunch and said that I should hang out with him sometimes, and he can tell me all about his project on the Sahara Desert that he's doing with Ms. Langies. I don't know why, but Samantha and Lillian and Yvette talk about me less when I'm with Sean. And Alex (Sean's best friend ever since Nathan went to the other class, which is my class now, I guess, and made friends with Pierce) gets along well enough with Momo and Nina.

The lunch Sean came over and told me to hang out with him, I was crying a little bit because of something Samantha said during class. He didn't make fun of me or anything, he just said when I was done crying that my eyes looked super green. I said that his eyes looked super brown and he said, "My eyes *are* brown."

I said, "And my eyes *are* green."

Then we talked about what we would do if we got stuck in the desert just the two of us, and we decided that we would never eat each other even if we were hungry. We said we would figure it out together. During class that afternoon, I felt a little bit tired and like I was all alone in the desert, but I think Sean decided to come with me, and now we're figuring it out, one day at a time. And, just because, Grandma Jen is there in the desert with us too.

Deserts aside, international week is coming up again, and I am so excited! There are forty-eight students this year in my grade, so none of us have to be Puerto Rico or Guam like they needed two kids to be last year. Mrs. N is teaching us for international week this year because Mr. Odber is bored with doing the same thing every year, and he and Mrs. N are friends, and he begged to be the one to teach fourth graders about France. She agreed, and she'll be in charge of half the fifth grade.

When Mrs. N came into the class today, I just about lost it. I just stood up and started applauding and soon everyone who had her last year was on their feet, and we were all clapping. She smiled real wide and said that she had missed us and then we all had to line up and give her hugs, but she hugged me the hardest, I think. (I realize that just because sometimes people can be tired and send you to the office, it doesn't mean they hate you. I think she feels bad about the way she was sometimes short with me last year.)

We got our states by choosing popsicle sticks. I drew California, which is great because I know how to make sand dunes out of clay now because of when I talked about the desert with Not-So-Stupid-Sean Hanner.

Mrs. N asked me to stay after class. She sat at Mr. Odber's desk wearing a red blouse and said, "I'm really proud of how quiet you've been in class today."

I said, "Thank you. I'm working on it."

She stared at me. "You seem a little bit sad, Miss W. You look like you might be tired."

"Oh," I said. "That's just because of all my medications."

"Are you happy with them?"

I didn't have answer. I don't know if I like them or not. "Mommy thinks they're helping."

Mrs. N nodded. "Okay. If you ever need someone to talk to, my door is always open."

I'm really glad Mrs. N is back. No one ever really asks me these days if I'm okay with the treatment, I just sort of have to do it. It made me feel like I was a person *with* a problem instead of the problem. You know?

After school, Mommy spent the whole afternoon taking pictures of the house, which she'd been doing, I guess, all day. She took pictures of the couch, kitchen, and the bedrooms (except mine and Ellie-An's because we refused to be a part of her new decorations) and then she did it all again at every stage of light in the day.

She would be all like, "The morning sun in the east strikes it just so, but the western afternoon sun is glorious, and sunset brings out the nature of openness."

I asked, "Does this lighting bring out my glass eye?"

Mommy said, "Yes, dear," because she wasn't really listening to me.

Grandma Jen decided the house was too crazy for her after spending the whole day in Mommy's out-of-the-blue picture palooza. She said today was the day she and I would try our final Baskin-Robbins flavor, so we left the house together. The last flavor was the black walnut, but I didn't really like it, so then we got soft-serve because we hadn't tried that, either, and we wanted to go out with a bang.

Speaking of bangs, Grandma Jen has recently begun to take a shooting class with Mr. Bennet. She got a gun license and everything and didn't tell anyone in the family. Daddy and I came into the kitchen a few days ago to see Grandma Jen holding a gun. We all just about flipped out, and Daddy was super big boy macho. He said, "Mom, give me the gun."

Well, Grandma Jen was having none of that and said, "There ain't no bullets, so shove off, Cameron." Then she explained about how it was Grandpa Claude's old shooting gun and how Mr. Bennet likes to shoot, too, so they were going hunting and now Grandma Jen renewed her license to carry a firearm.

Daddy said that Grandma Jen was crazy, and she said, "Darn straight," so I had to cover my ears again and said that swearing was bad for my development. Grandma Jen laughed and said maybe it was character building. Daddy said that I could be in the army.

I said, "Maybe I can if Grandma Jen teaches me how to shoot."

Grandma Jen said, "You're too young right now, but I'll teach when you get to eighth grade."

I have something to look forward to, and I'll wait until then.

Speaking of growing up, when I was in fourth grade, I wanted to be a bee. I wanted to be a powerful woman who would push out men every winter and spend her life as part of a hive, a group of people all working together. Now that I am older, I want to be a swimmer. I want to be part of a team of strong women working together like bees in a hive. I want that and so does Coach Summers. He's been saying now at every practice that I've got a shot and something bigger than even competition swimming. He told me that if I ever win two meets in every category that he'll talk to my parents about the national team. He told me that I could go to the Olympics someday if I train hard enough. It's really cool that I have something I'm just good at, somewhere I don't get yelled out for being who I am.

Speaking of people who like me for who I am, a few days ago Momo and I walked over the Hoan (a bridge in Milwaukee that I love, but I bet you knew that) together just for funsies, but when we were in the middle, Momo was all like, "I'm falling in love!"

This was just too exciting, so I said, "Who? Who?" Momo was being secretive, and she just kept saying, "Someone."

I said, "But who someone?"

She was like, "Someone I know someone."

I decided that the game was stupid, and she didn't really like anyone. I said, "Good for you," in the way that Grandma Jen says, "Good for you, Cameron," when she thinks something has happened to Daddy that really isn't very good at all, and then I kept walking.

Momo really did want to tell me because then she said, "No, wait, I have a crush on Alex." And I was super shocked because Alex is like just so not cute for me. I mean, I guess I think blonds are kinda weird in general because my dad is blond.

I said, "Alex as in blond Sean's friend?"

Momo blushed the color of my jacket, and I was just so taken aback that I couldn't even talk, which I'll tell you is a huge deal.

I whispered, "But Nina's into the same Alex."

Momo got this dreamy smile. "I can share."

She said we had to make a wish for something on top of that bridge, and she was wishing for love, and I could wish for anything and it would come true. So while she wished for love, I wished to someday wake up and not worry about focusing or anything but just feel okay in my skin. And you know, now that I know what I really wish for, I feel like maybe it'll get easier, just a little bit, day by day. I'm not shooting for perfection—I'm working toward alright.

Sincerely,

A Girl with a Wish

Dear the Man Upstairs,

Yesterday, Mommy got her first client for her now home-service decoration thing. The person who hired her is an old rich lady who lives in New York City and wants to bring the whole living house thing to the big city.

Mommy kept on looking stuff up online and writing out huge lists of things on individual Post-it notes and sticking them all over the windows. Daddy asked her why she couldn't just write stuff down on the computer or get bigger Post-it notes, and she said that every artist has her process.

Grandma Jen has been having a good old time taking off the Post-it notes when Mommy isn't looking and replacing them with things that say, "buy some more orange juice," or "change Ellie-An's diaper" instead of what might have been actually written, "match green with powder blue and hints of lavender." Daddy's also been writing his own Post-its, so sometimes Mommy goes to check her notes and sees things like, "I love you," or "let's Netflix and chill when the kids are asleep."

This last note I found particularly rude because I enjoy watching TV when I have time, and I think my parents should absolutely not be allowed to watch TV after I am asleep. In one more month, Ellie-An and me will have to start sharing a room, but until then, Ellie-An sleeps in Mommy and Daddy's room. So I guess Mommy and Daddy would have to chill in the living room? I've taken to writing my own Post-it notes, ones that will say, "Have a good day," or "Best of Luck, Mommy," and things like that.

Mommy has been thanking Daddy and me a bunch for our notes, but she keeps on getting mad at Grandma Jen. Now there are Post-it notes all over Grandma Jen's room that Mommy writes, and they say things like, "growing old but not growing up," and "your heart is in the wrong place." This really scared me.

I tried to ask Mommy if Grandma Jen's heart wasn't in the right place, where was it? "Mommy? Where is Grandma Jen's heart? Hearts are really important. We've been learning about how they are muscles in science class. She'll die if it's not in her chest!"

Mommy said, "What? Grandma Jen's heart is fine."

"But *where* is it?" I asked again. Mommy just looked super confused.

Daddy's gotten annoyed at all the notes and said, "Will you two stop this petty fight?"

I don't think hearts in wrong places are petty. They're dangerous.

I tried to ask Ms. Pepper, Mr. Odber's assistant who is now helping Mrs. N during the preparations for international week, what it means to have your heart not be in the right place. Ms. Pepper said, "Miss W, I need you to stop getting so off topic."

Samantha laughed too loudly at me even though the comment Ms. Pepper made wasn't very funny.

Mrs. N is more observant than Mr. Odber. She told Samantha, "that was not very kind. Please stay after class to talk to me." Samantha slouched down in her seat. I kind of related to her because I've been asked that same question more than once.

Mrs. N said to me, "When someone says 'your heart is in the right place,' it means that they think you are trying to do what's right, even if you're not actually doing the best thing."

I turned this over in my head. "Does that mean that having your heart in the wrong place means you're trying to do a bad thing and instead are accidentally doing a good thing?"

"I don't know," Mrs. N said.

I got home from school and learned that Mommy's new designs are good. (I could have told you that. Of course, Mommy is talented, she made Ellie-An, the greatest credit to mankind ever even if she cries too much.) Mommy got her very first paycheck yesterday, and she's super excited. It's the first time she's made any money since I was born. Daddy was super proud of her and made her a fancy dinner (not really, he bought food from Olive Garden but it was still a good try) and I ate the breadsticks and Mommy got all emotional.

Grandma Jen said she'd take us all out to healthy smoothies to celebrate, and Mommy said that would be great because "being healthy is important, Jen, I'm glad you understand." We went to that same juice place Mommy brought me to before my sister was born, and we all ordered things that will keep us young forever with shiny hair and strong nails.

Grandma Jen brought Mr. Bennet. I've only ever seen him when he takes his tiny dogs on walks around the neighborhood. I'd never talked to him. I cornered him by the edge of the restaurant to ask him some important questions because I knew that Daddy wouldn't, and someone needs to protect Grandma Jen. Just because he looks like a harmless grandpa who wears shirts that say, $X+7=10$, find X and the "X" is circled in red, which is funny, and seems good at giving hugs, it doesn't mean he is that kind of grandpa.

I looked up into his soft blue eyes and past all his smile lines and well-worn wrinkles and asked him, "Do you like chocolate?"

He said, very seriously, "I do. But I prefer lemon."

I puzzled this over for a long moment. "Do you like headscarves?"

His face did this weird thing where it looked really sad and a little bit fond. "Yes," he said quietly. "But I do not like what they represent."

I didn't know what to say to that, so I put it away for later and asked, "Do you love Grandma Jen?"

He smiled then and beamed over to where Grandma Jen was holding Ellie-An on her lap and looking at the two of us like we were her whole world. Ellie-An blew bubbles of kale juice all over Mommy's pants and it was glorious.

"I do," he said in a whisper. "I really do."

Sincerely,

Miss W

PS

Mr. Bennet is alright in my books.

Dear Miss W,

I'm sorry for writing to you less frequently. I've been busy trying to heal from some things, and I'm afraid my letters might start to take longer to get to you. I would still love to hear from you, even if I don't always respond.

It sounds like Mrs. N is trying to do her best by you. I am so glad you have a teacher who is stepping in. Samantha seems like she could learn to treat others with the respect all people deserve. From what I can tell, it would appear that you are going through a little bit of a tough time and could benefit from reaching out to a trusted adult. I know you want to be happy all the time, but it is okay to need help. You are adjusting to medication, and that must be challenging.

Some days, it is okay to be sad. Crying is just as an important part of life as laughing. After your grandfather died, your Grandma Jen kept smiling. She would pretend to everyone that she was as good as ever, but then she would break down alone, and the people she loved would find her sitting in the darkness with red eyes and cheeks pinched in the least-believable smile you've ever seen. You take after her in so many ways, but you do not need to weather the storm alone.

Humans aren't made to feel only one emotion. There's a lot of beauty in how many moods a person can have, just like how a rainbow has red and purple and all the in-between.

Just because you feel happy and red most days doesn't mean that waking up purple or blue every now and again will change who you are. Each and every person is endowed with an entire rainbow, and how you feel doesn't change just how spectacular you truly are.

Warmly,
the Man Upstairs

Dear the Man Upstairs,

Red is a happy and vibrant color, so I *am* red most of the time. I really like your rainbow thing; it feels pretty cool and I'm totally stealing it at some point and using it for school because it's super deep too. I actually said to Grandma Jen when she asked me how I was doing that I was feeling purple, and I feel like she kinda got it because she looked sad for me, but she asked me what I meant by purple, anyways, because I think she could tell I was unhappy but didn't totally understand the metaphor.

I also told Momo I was feeling purple, but Momo didn't get it at all. She said that purple is pretty but that she was feeling extra red because "red is the color of love" and Momo is still in love. Nina decided she was feeling yellow because she really likes dandelions and has decided that yellow is now her favorite color.

Why does everyone always say, "How are you?" I don't get it. People only want you to say "good" so they can move on with their lives. Now when I give them a color (and by them, I mean the adults who I know, like teachers and some of Dad's beer and basketball friends) they get all confused and don't really want to ask me another question but also don't want to feel like they're missing something. Why ask in the first place if you don't care?

Mrs. N asked about me and did care, and I told her that I was feeling purple. She asked me what I meant, and I said that people were rainbows and that red to purple is happiness to sadness and then she said how could she help maybe get me up to blue or even green today?

I said, "Could you maybe tell me something you like about me?"

Mrs. N looked at me with big eyes and this soft smile. "I really love how much you try to help out your friends."

That made me feel warm inside. I do try to help out my friends, like I helped Momo write a love letter she'll never send to Alex, and I helped Nina with her math homework. It's nice that someone notices.

Oh! Here's the letter I helped Momo write:

Dear Alex,

Your dimples are deeper than the Mariana Trench. Your sandy hair is fuller than the beach of the Atlantic. Your blue-green eyes reflect the secrets of the ocean. Your glorious heart lives to be entrenched in love.

I can be your sea vent, keeping you warm in the dark. I can be your seashells nestled in your sand. I will be your fishies, swimming and giving your ocean life. I can be the person to give your heart the love it needs to survive.

I am Momo, the girl who sits next to your friend Sean Hanner, and I am the girl who will lead us all to victory in international week. I enjoy knitting and cooking, so I'll probably be a decent wife.

My parents don't approve of boys yet because I'm not allowed to date anyone until I'm thirty, but my cousin is a makeup artist so we could trick them into thinking you are a girl for the next twenty years until you propose and then we can be like, "Surprise! He's been a boy this whole time and you guys are invited to the wedding."

I know that all this information may seem a little bit like too much, but I am a woman of commitment. I would not want us to enter a relationship without the proper knowledge.

I think you're super cute and really sweet, and I really want to be your girlfriend. Will you be my first boyfriend?

Heart,

Momo

I only helped with the last two sentences. Momo got lots of help from her cousin (yes the makeup artist).

It was super fun to see and read, and it made me think about nothing but Momo and Alex (and Nina, because Nina is still into Alex and that seems like a recipe for disaster) for an afternoon.

But all good things must end, Daddy always says, so today I had a meeting with Dr. Keaty about fifth grade. She was checking in to make sure all my new strategies were working. To be clear, they are working okay. I mean I am tired sometimes, but sometimes I am awake. I can focus better, but not as well as Momo. I mean, I think I'm normal but doesn't everyone?

Anyways, after a boring meeting without a Snickers or even a Hershey's Kiss, Grandma Jen took me out to ice cream again. We were sitting down on the red benches, enjoying some carefully scooped Mexican coco-nib ice-cream, when Grandma Jen got all serious.

She tells me, "Darling, I've got something you need to know."

I say, "Well, what is it?"

She says, "It isn't good. In fact, it is very bad."

I say, a little bit nervous, "Okay." I wasn't sure what she was going to say. My heart was beating quickly.

Then she says, "Sweetheart, you know how a few weeks ago I went to the doctor?"

I said, "Yeah," because she's been going an awful lot lately.

She took my hands in hers. "Well, I got some blood tests, and they came back positive. I've been trying to figure out how to break the news to you since your swim meet."

I said, "Okay," again because that was all I could manage.

And then she said, "I have breast cancer."

So then I asked the question I just had to ask: "But you'll be okay, right? Like the doctors can fix it and you'll be back in no time?"

She didn't say yes.

She said, "The doctors aren't sure right now if it's spread at all. There's a good chance we caught it early enough, but sometimes, the cancer can spread quickly even when it's caught early."

"Will anything change right now?" I asked.

She shook her head, and I couldn't stop looking at her headscarf. "Not really. the doctors need to run some more tests, and I'll start getting some treatments."

"Is that why you're wearing headscarves?"

Grandma Jen took a shaky breath. "Sort of. I still have all my hair. I just started wearing these because when I start treatments, I will lose all of it and I want to… I want to still feel beautiful if… if that does happen."

"You will look beautiful no matter what happens," I promised.

We drove back together to the house. I told her, "I love you so much. You're the best grandmother in the whole world." And then I ran upstairs to my room. I grabbed Mr. Wiggles the stuffed bear, and I looked at Ellie-An's empty crib that she'll move into when she's big enough, and I started to cry. What kind of world just lets someone as good as Grandma Jen get sick? Why couldn't bad people get sick, like Al Capone, or Daddy's boss? How is it fair?

It *isn't* fair.

When I was crying, Mommy came into the room, and she just hugged me on my bed. She didn't even say anything about the mess of clean laundry on the floor.

She just said, "It's hard, baby. I know. I know." And I think that she does know. Because for all that she and Grandma Jen argue, they do love each other at the end of the day. And I hope that they'll love each other tomorrow, too, because I refuse to believe that someone as strong as Grandma Jen is gonna be taken down by some cancer. Maybe that could happen to someone else's grandma but not to mine.

- Miss W

Dear the Man Upstairs,

Daddy decided to take the day off from work and take me fishing. I don't really know what he was thinking. For as long as I have been alive, I have not enjoyed the smell of fish. I don't really know how to describe how much I hate fish, but I'll try. Imagine the feeling of going into the dark for food in your refrigerator, trying to pull out an apple, and instead coming out with week-old molded cream cheese. That is how I feel about fish.

But Daddy brought me fishing, anyway. He's been spending more time with me recently, and even if we don't always do my favorite things, hanging out with Daddy *is* one of my favorite things.

We sat on the water, in a staring contest, both of our lines over Grandpa Claude's old blue rowboat. I felt a tug and so I spun the spinner fast as it would go. I began to pull the fish out from the lake, and then I realized that I had caught a flip-flop.

Daddy raised an eyebrow at me. "That'll make a great dinner."

Daddy felt a tug and pulled out a soda can.

"That will make a fabulous dessert," I said.

A little later, Daddy caught a real fish, just it was so small we felt bad and let it go back into the lake. But then it was lunchtime, so Daddy rowed us to shore, and we ate peanut butter and jelly sandwiches with blackberry jam and crunchy peanut butter, which is just how I like it.

I told Daddy, "If the whole writing grants thing doesn't work out, you could make sandwiches for a living."

Daddy swallowed his bite of food. "I could. Wouldn't be much of a living, though."

I smoothed my hands against my jeans. "You could always go work in a planetarium."

"I don't know why I would do that. I have a job, Miss W. I already met my own Grandma Jen years ago, and now I have my own baby Cameron and Matthias. I've got…I've gotten to have this beautiful family." Daddy got a little teary eyed and pulled me forward on the picnic blanket and into a real tight hug. I could feel him crying just a little bit. Daddy never cries.

It made me remember that Grandma Jen is my grandmother, but she was his mommy first. I turned my face into his shoulder and pretended that Daddy's big shoulders could protect me from everything that's falling apart.

Grandma Jen keeps on going to the doctors. Mr. Bennet (he told me to call him Grandpa Q because his name is Quincey) takes her every time, and sometimes he drives me to Dr. Keaty. Grandma Jen goes three times a week for radiation, but she still lives at home. She gets tired and angry more easily than she used to, and she's off Ellie-An duty. It's my job to feed my little sister gross formula from the bottle.

Just the other day, I started feeding her milk, and she thought it would be funny if she blew a raspberry. All over me her half-sipped milk went, but as I was wiping off the stuff, she started to copy me. She kept smoothing the milk into her hair and all over her face. She doesn't have the same body control that I do.

I had to go get her a wet warm towel, and I rubbed her little face clean, and she just sat there giggling. Of course, there was still more milk for her to drink, so then I tried feeding her again, but she wasn't really interested in eating. She pushed the bottle away, and then she grabbed my fingers and tried to suck on them! I tried to take them back but then she started to cry. So I quickly washed my hands and gave her my left pinky finger because it's the finger I love the least, and I let her suck on it like it was a pacifier. Love makes us fools, Gampa always says.

Mommy came into the kitchen, and she took Ellie-An to put her down for a nap, but I don't think she really noticed how well I had taken care of her. When she got back from her bedroom, I told her all about the sucking on my fingers like she was a vampire, and then Mommy started laughing.

"She does do that, doesn't she?" Mommy asked.

"I didn't know!" I was laughing so you could barely understand me. "This was the first time I ever fed her!" Mommy started laughing too.

Then she said, "You were the same way." She gave me a little pat on the head. "You know, you're still my baby."

And I didn't know, so I'm glad she told me.

Sincerely,

Miss W, the Best Older Sister Known to Man, a Girl Worried about Her Grandmother

Dear Miss W,

It takes incredible strength to continue to move forward when someone we love is sick. All the emotions you are feeling and will feel—the sadness, anger, despair, love, exhaustion— are worth feeling, even when they hurt.

Whatever happens to your grandmother will never be your fault. You need to know that. Your news is hard for me, too. I have been your grandmother's friend for a long time.

We got to know each other very well, she and I, and so I wish her all the health in the world. Unfortunately, you and I don't have that power. We'll just have to wish her all the best and believe in our hearts that she is strong enough to pull through. Your family will be there to support you every step of the way, just like I know you will be there to support them.

No matter what happens, she will remain strong enough to love you, and I bet that you will stay strong enough to love her. She's full of love, that Grandma Jen of yours, and that is what you should always remember.

Condolences,
the Man Upstairs

Dear the Man Upstairs,

I am sad and everything, feeling awful purple these days, but do I know that Grandma Jen loves me a bunch. She knows that I love her too. I guess it's been so long talking to you that I kinda forgot we met through Grandma Jen and that she was your friend too. I guess you must be pretty old, huh? Does it ever get boring talking to a little kid like me? Are you worried about her, too?

One time I don't worry about her is when I swim. The pool is great because it has no homework, no teachers, and no banana slugs that I can use to scare Stupid Sean Hanner. The pool, in fact, has no Sean Hanner at all.

Just the other day in the pool, Mon asked me when Sean and I were getting married, because we're clearly in love and I talk about him all the time. I told him he sounded just like

Momo, and he said that he hadn't ever met Momo, but she seemed like a smart girl.

I said that she was but he wasn't, and he said of course, he wasn't, because he's a boy. He was all like, "I'm a smart boy, though, I'm just not a smart girl."

I said, "I guess that's true," and pushed off the wall. I swam a bunch of laps faster than most of the seventh graders. They seem a little bit jealous of me sometimes. (It's not the worst feeling. It's nice to be good at something.)

When Mon and I took a little break, he said, "Do you want to hear a joke?" I think he could tell I was upset about something even though I haven't told him about how Grandma Jen is sick.

I said, "Yes, please."

He said, "Why was the salad embarrassed when the boy opened the refrigerator door?"

I said, "Why?"

He said, "Because she was undressed!"

I laughed a little bit because that made me feel better and then I knocked him in the shoulder. "Thanks, Mon."

He tapped me in the center of my forehead. "Anytime, swimmer-girl."

Sincerely,

Miss W, Mon's Swimmer-Girl

Dear the Man Upstairs,

After swimming, Mr. Bennet invited me to his house and told me that he wanted my help in proposing to Grandma Jen. They've only known each other six months now, but I guess that was enough time for him to really fall in love.

The plan is that he will invite me out to ice cream, and Grandma Jen will come with us. Then, while Grandma

Jen orders ice cream, he will hand me the ring he bought her. He says that he'll ask Grandma Jen to go on a little walk with him, and he'll ask me to carry the ice creams while he and Grandma Jen find a nice place to sit outside. While they're walking in front of me, I'll stick the ring in Grandma Jen's ice cream. We'll decide to sit in front of the lake that's right by the Baskin-Robbins at sunset, and she'll eat her ice cream and find the ring. He'll get down on one knee and propose, and Daddy will come and get me, and we'll leave them alone. Grandma Jen and Mr. Bennet will watch the stars come out over the lake, and it'll be like their own planetarium.

I am very excited to be a part of the plan. Grandma Jen really likes Mr. Bennet, and she also likes Fifi, the little dog Mr. Bennet (who really wants me to call him Grandpa Q) has a hard time walking. Grandma Jen deserves to have a man who loves her the way Grandpa Claude loved her, and even though I never met Grandpa Claude, I think that Mr. Bennet may just be that man. I was telling Momo about the whole plan in class because we're about to present during international week, and we sit next to each other during project time now that both classes are working together. She told me I should sneak in some cinnamon to Grandma Jen's ice cream because "cinnamon is the spice of love," but I told her that was just plain weird. She shrugged her shoulders and said, "I am just plain weird. But so is love."

Ugh, Mon was also talking about love when I told him about it. Mon and Momo need to chill out. Not everything is a romance novel. But I wouldn't really know; I haven't read any. If you ask Grandma Jen, Mommy's read them all.

Mon finally told us why he's always so lifeless on Mondays. His parents don't live together anymore, so he has to move between their houses. He actually spends weekends with his way-older brother, who he really loves, and his dad, but they live all the way in Chicago, which is in a whole other state and a four-hour drive away. So he always leaves late on Sunday night and often gets back home when it's already Monday, so no wonder he's so tired.

I guess that it's really hard when your parents don't live together, so then I went home and asked Mommy and Daddy to keep living together and they gave me the "Are you crazy? You really just might be" look so I gave them the "I am about to be a teenager and am infinitely cooler than you" look and then Grandma Jen gave us the "I am the adult, and I am bored of this so stop of all of your looks" look.

I'm going to tell you something that is kind of off topic, but I swear it will make sense. Do you ever like, really have to go to the bathroom, except you're in the middle of something super important and really just don't want to? Do you ever feel like maybe if you just went to sleep a little bit later somehow everything you feel like you should have gotten done will just suddenly happen? No, just me? I don't know. I guess maybe I'm feeling both right now.

Do you know that when I was a little bit younger than I am now I could get lost going places? Like this one time I got lost in a shoe store because I went out the back door to find the bathroom but got distracted by another little girl who had a balloon, so I followed her balloon and then by the time she went away with her parents, I realized that I had no idea where my parents were.

I was a smart kid and everything, so I went to the nearest safe-looking adult, a woman with a purple baby carriage, and told her I was lost and would she please call my parents.

She was all like, "Oh, my goodness, yes, of course, sweetie," and then Mommy came and was super freaked out and angry and the whole shebang.

Well, sometimes I think back on how scared Mommy must have been, but the truth is that I was never scared at all. I was doing something the whole time, and it isn't likely that someone would steal me away in front of a Payless shoe store in a little mall in the middle of the summer. I think that maybe I'm like Mommy right now, and Grandma Jen is like me. She's doing all the work of getting treatments, and she doesn't seem that scared. She's doing something the whole time. It's hard to be the person waiting and hoping everything will turn out alright.

That being said, sometimes I can feel myself following the balloon, and I know that if I keep on, I might get lost. So I really need to use the bathroom and stop thinking about the word "look" and be a better friend and a better older sister because Ellie-An is probably sad that I'm not paying attention to her, but me writing this to you has been my way of following the balloon and doing something so I don't think too hard about Grandma Jen.

Sincerely,
Miss W

Dear the Man Upstairs,

Today is the day Mr. Bennet will propose to Grandma Jen. I'm wearing my best dress and everything. Wish Grandma Jen and me good luck. I'll tell you all about it after they're engaged.

Sincerely,
Miss W

Dear the Man Upstairs,

I think when people are in love, they understand the little things really well. Daddy can tell when Mommy is angry just by the kind of flat smile she gives him, which is something I'm not good at figuring out yet. (Dr. Keaty says understanding facial expressions is a growth-area for me, but that's beside the point.)

Even though I'd totally kept the proposal a secret from Grandma Jen, she took extra time getting ready and doing her makeup and putting on an extra nice scarf. (Her hair is starting to fall out now.) She must have picked up on all the little things to tell her it was going to be a special day, but for all she knew, we were just getting ice cream. Maybe she just really wanted to look nice for Mr. Bennet, but I think it would be awfully romantic if she could just tell something wonderful was on its way.

When Mr. Bennet offered to drive us all (me, Daddy, and Grandma Jen) to the Baskin-Robbins she said, "Absolutely," and she even had a blush, which stood out brightly on her skin because it's been paler these days. I think that Mr. Bennet (Call me Grandpa Q for the love of God) and Grandma Jen might actually just be in love. She ordered us all a big sundae to share, which was perfect, because then I could hold it on the walk we were going to take and not have to worry about having four cones in my two hands, which would have happened if she'd ordered something for just herself. While she was ordering, Mr. Bennet slipped the ring into my pocket, and I gave him a thumbs up. Daddy ruffled my hair.

Grandma Jen came back with a hot fudge sundae dripping in caramel sauce, and that's my favorite. Grandma Jen said, "It's kind of loud in here, Quincey."

Mr. Bennet couldn't have found a better opening if he tried so he said, "Well, then let's find a place to sit outside." The sun was just beginning to set. Mr. Bennet led Grandma Jen on a short walk to the edge of the lake and then he set down his jacket and asked her to sit like he was a proper gentleman. While they were doing their thing, Daddy gave me a nudge, and I put the ring on the sundae.

Grandma Jen sat down, and I swear she blushed a little *again*. I came over and handed her the sundae with my most innocent smile so she wouldn't know anything was going to happen. Proposals are supposed to be nice surprises, like Christmas presents, and not bad surprises like spoiled yogurt in your lunchbox. (Sometimes Mommy swears that my lunchbox is growing a new lifeform.)

So Grandma Jen goes to take her first bite of the ice cream, but there on the spoon is a ring. Mr. Bennet goes down on one knee and says, "These past few months of being with you have been my sweetest. Would you do me the honor of being my wife?"

Grandma Jen just started crying and so Mr. Bennet stopped kneeling and settled down on his jacket beside her and hugged around her shoulders real tight. Daddy wrapped his arms around *my* shoulders and brought me away saying we had to let them have their own space. Dads, am I right?

I don't know yet what happened afterward. All I know is as we were leaving, the sun was setting, and the stars began to break free and shoot across the sky as brilliant lights, and that each and every one reflected up on Grandma Jen from the lake.

Sincerely,
Miss W
PS

Momo told me that Grandma Jen became a constellation of love, whatever that means. Mon said that Momo has the most sense of anyone that he's never met. Nina just said she was happy for me.

Dear the Man Upstairs,

Mr. Bennet and Grandma Jen are officially getting married, but we don't know when just yet. Also, annoyingly, there is a boy named Quincey in my class (he wears tinfoil hats) and I keep getting confused if people are talking about him or Mr. Bennet. Who knew Quincey was such a common name?

Anyways, Mr. Bennet has two daughters, and apparently neither of them really knew how much he liked Grandma Jen. They came to visit in order to meet their soon-to-be new mom because they want to make sure that Grandma Jen is a good person or something. Like duh, of course she is. She literally volunteers at the church sandwich hunger project. Do you think bad people make hundreds of peanut butter and jelly sandwiches for hungry children without eating them at all every single Sunday? Because spoiler alert: they don't. I mean Grandma Jen can be a bit of a bully sometimes, but I think everyone can be a bit of a bully sometimes. What matters is how you are most of the time. Right? Right.

Grr. And also, one of Mr. Bennet's (who's started saying, "for all the good things in the world, would you PLEASE call me Grandpa Q?") daughters has a daughter my age. Everyone is acting like the two of us are gonna be best friends or something.

I don't think I like her very much. I already have three best friends: Nina, Momo, and Mon. I don't need a fourth. I mean, if we become friends, that's great. I just don't think it's a good idea to try and make people be friends. You can't force friendship. That's what Dr. Keaty says, anyway.

Mrs. N is no longer teaching our class, and Mr. Odber is back because international week is over. It's March already. My presentation on California lasted exactly two minutes and nobody from home could come because Grandma Jen was at the doctor's and Grandpa Q was with her, and Mommy had to take care of Ellie-An and Daddy had to be at a meeting.

I was pretty sad about it, actually, and I still am. But it's not as if I had a dance recital this time or anything. And Mrs. N said she was proud of me. I'm trying not to think about it too hard, how no one came this year. Samantha and Yvette asked if no one cared about me and if everyone had given up on me, but then Yerena, Nina's mom, said that she was there for me as much as Nina, and then she complained about Samantha and Yvette to Vice Principal Viceport. Now I think that the fifth-grade girls are going to have to go to an anti-bullying talk because I heard Mr. Odber talking about with Ms. Pepper, his assistant.

"Bully" is one of those words that can get lost in your head and rattle around and not make much sense. Grandma Jen can be a bit of a bully to Mommy, sometimes, but she's not trying to be mean. And I think that Samantha is trying to be mean, so it feels like something else altogether.

I worry that sometimes I'm an easy target because there's so many things I do that you can make fun of, and I know that it's not my fault people make fun of me, but sometimes it can *feel* that way. I definitely felt that way when I did my presentation in front of a bunch of people who didn't love me and found myself looking for my family only to come face to face with a mean Samantha and Yvette.

But that was last week, and this week, Grandpa Q's daughters came into town. One of them is named Lacey, and she's eight and a half years younger than Beatrice, her older sister. Mr. Bennet clearly really loves them both. Beatrice has THE daughter who is also ten and her name is Jeanette.

When they got into town, my family and Grandpa Q's family decided that we should all go out to dinner. We went to an Italian restaurant. Almost as soon as we sat down, Beatrice was loudly telling Jeanette to talk to me and make friends with "your short cousin." This was a weird thing for her to do, because Jeanette was clearly so much more interested in her phone than in having a conversation with me.

Beatrice was all like, "No phones at the table," and I guess Jeanette interpreted this to mean "the phones must go under the table." She spent all this time looking down at her pants and playing some dumb game with candy on her smartphone. I wished, though maybe it made me a bully, that I was sitting farther away from her.

I don't have a smartphone yet because Mommy says I don't need one. We were learning in school that people can get addicted to screens and then you get less smart. I felt kinda bad for Jeanette, actually, because she was setting herself up for a life-long addiction the whole time she was playing the candy game, and she didn't even know it. Beatrice's husband couldn't come to meet Grandma Jen, but Lacey's husband did, and his name was Brett.

Brett was super cool. When he first met me, he said I had something behind my ear and pulled out a coin. When he snapped, the coin turned into a flower. He's trying to become a magician, but Mr. Bennet kept on asking him how medical school was going. I guess he's going to graduate in a few months, and then he'll stay on at his position at the hospital in somewhere, somewhere.

Lacey seemed really interested in Grandma Jen. She asked all about everything, like favorite colors and movies and if Grandma Jen was a cat or dog person.

Grandma Jen said, "People person." I thought it was a good answer, but it seemed to confuse the heck out of Lacey.

The next day, Mommy and I went to the park with the extended almost-family. Daddy stayed home after saying that he "can watch Ellie-An sometimes too." It turns out that I really just cannot stand Beatrice. All she ever wants to do is pass off Jeanette to me, and it's clearly not because she wants us to be friends like I first thought, but because she has other things she wants to do.

We all got to the park and then, as soon as Jeanette and I seem to be mildly involved with one another, like we are walking ten feet apart in the same general direction, Beatrice (Jeanette's *mother*) is all like, "Oh my gosh, I'm so sorry, I forgot I have this appointment." And then at dinner, she had shiny nails and glossy hair, so I'm guessing her "appointments" were for herself and not for work. At least when Mommy has appointments, they're with Expat or Ermengarde, her newest client. She attracts all the rich and weird old ladies, but I'm not complaining. She's made a profit this year, so all the new house stuff is totally paid for. Daddy said that she's actually making enough money that we might go on vacation next winter. That would be super exciting because we never go anywhere.

Anyways, as soon as Beatrice left the park, Jeanette was texting her friends and trying to find a way to leave and go to some person's house who she had met online. I was all like "stranger danger," and "I bet you the person you're texting is not a cool twelve-year-old-boy but actually some creepy man older than Mr. Bennet and interested in girls much younger than him, even more than according to Mommy, Daddy's boss is interested in younger women."

She tossed her black hair over one shoulder and said, "You're just jealous because you have no game and are still a little kid."

I said, "I'm still alive, I'm already eleven, and I'm even an Olympic hopeful." That wasn't really true, but I wanted to show off a little because, honestly, I am pretty childish and even though I'm not trying to be popular or dating boys, it's not as if I'm stupid. I know that's what a lot of kids want to be, popular and cool, and sometimes I can't help but feel the same way too.

Jeanette was all like, "No way you're an Olympic hopeful. And even if you are, I'm the fastest girl in my PE class. I bet you can't beat me in a running race."

"I'm an Olympic hopeful in *swimming,* not running. I don't know if I would be able to—"

"If you're a *real* athlete," Jeanette cut me off, "you should be able to win doing any sport. Or are you scared you'll lose?"

I squared my shoulders. "Fine, let's race. I'm just saying, this is not my sport."

She smirked. "Get ready to lose."

I felt kinda nervous. I've never really run because we start doing the mile next year in PE. "How far do you want to race."

She said, "To the end of the park," which was about as long as eight trees. "I want Aunt Lacey to be the judge because I don't trust anyone from *your* family to be a fair judge. And if I win, I want you to admit that you're a baby."

That didn't sound so bad. I'm not a baby, and I know that Mommy would just roll her eyes and say, "No, you're not."

"Okay," I said. "If I win, I want you to show the adults about the boy you're texting because I'm worried about you."

Jeanette spit, "Fine."

We got into position on the grass. Lacey counted to three and then we were sprinting across the grass. I had taken off my shoes and the mud was just tumbling out behind me. It turns out that I can run a lot faster than I can swim, and I guess it's true that when you are good at one sport, you are good at a lot of them. At first, Jeanette was ahead of me, but I passed her like a third of the way to the end of the park and I kept gaining. She ended up finishing the race a full three seconds behind me, and if you're a swimmer who competes like me, you know that's a lot of time.

Jeanette really wants to race me in swimming now, because she's somehow convinced herself that she could beat me at what I do best. I don't want to burst her bubble, but I got moved up an entire age category, and I could probably go to the national team if I wanted to. Coach Summers said that I'm joining his elites next semester.

Instead, I just asked her, "Please show your phone to Lacey."

Jeanette glared at me. "I won't show her my phone, and you can't make me."

She was holding her phone in one hand, and Lacey walked over and plucked it out of Jeanette's fingers. "Show me what?"

"Nothing," Jeanette said.

Lacey said, "That's not suspicious at all," and called Beatrice. Beatrice told Lacey Jeanette's passcode because apparently Beatrice is allowed to know everything about everything when it comes to Jeanette.

Jeanette's profile and that other twelve-year-old boy came up, and Lacey's face went all white and she said something like, "You know this boy probably isn't even the age that he says he is. This is super dangerous."

Apparently, she and Jeanette and Beatrice are going to have to have a conversation. Kind of like the anti-bullying talk the fifth grade is going to have, but less for the good of everyone, and more for the safety of just one person. Jeanette was kind of angry with me, but at dinner that night with Mr. Bennet, it was clear that both Lacey and Beatrice like me more now. I was a hero today, Man Upstairs. I'm pretty sure that I may just have saved someone's life. Even though she is kind of stupid.

Sincerely,

Miss W, the Fifth-Grade Superhero

Dear Miss W,

I am impressed with you for recognizing danger and acting in an appropriate manner. I have complete confidence that even sick and feverish, you could beat your soon-to-be cousin in a swim race. Perhaps by even more than a full three seconds, if you ask me.

Warmly,

the Man Upstairs

Dear the Man Upstairs,

Thank you for believing in me. I think you are probably right, but then again, everyone wants to think that they are amazing. Not so many people really are. Daddy said that Jeanette wants people to think she's amazing, but she's probably just insecure. (Mommy told Daddy to stop gossiping about his new almost-family, and Daddy said, "I am who I am.")

I kind of understand Jeanette because I'm insecure about a lot of things, too, but I wish she wouldn't take it out on people. She needs to go to the anti-bullying talk with me, I think, but she's not part of my school. Beatrice decided to excuse Jeanette from her school for a few weeks for this visit because, "What do you really learn in fifth grade, anyway?"

I didn't tell her that we learn all about fractions and the American Revolution because that didn't seem to be the kind of thing she'd want to hear.

Yesterday, Mr. Bennet asked me to come and talk to him, and he and my whole family (not his) had a little get together at our house. He said he knew that his daughters weren't always the most loving people at first, but they have good intentions. I guess that when Lacey was four and Beatrice twelve, his wife died. He said, "Losing Jenna was hard on them both, but especially on Beatrice. She really pulled her weight for the family hard, taking care of Lacey. She tried her best to be a mother, but she didn't have a mother. But now that she has her own child, sometimes I think she wants to be the child she never got to be. She has ups and downs, but I hope that you all can understand. After all, we are going to be family soon, I hope."

Mommy said, "Of course, we understand, Quincey. How awful it would be to lose a mother."

Daddy and Grandma Jen squeezed each other's hands. I think they were thinking about Grandpa Claude. He didn't die because he got sick or anything, but Grandma Jen doesn't like to talk about it, and Daddy still says it's a sore subject for him. I think maybe that's also why Mr. Bennet (Grandpa Q?) and Grandma Jen are such a good pair. They both understand the sadness of losing someone you love when they're too young to die.

I'm really grateful that no one in my family is dead or going to die, at least not until I'm at least a real adult with children all the way in college. (Grandma Jen will get better, right?) I'll have to be older than my parents are right now and then some before it will be okay for Mommy and Daddy to die. If you ask me, it will never be okay at all.

After Mr. Bennet left, I told them, and they both laughed and said they would be around until I was sick of them. I said I was already sick of them, I just would be so much sicker without them.

Daddy said, "When we go, you'll have Ellie-An and a whole family of your own," and then he looked at me and Ellie-An and Mommy and said, "Like I do right now."

Mommy sniffled and I asked, "But Grandma Jen isn't going to go, right? She's going to be okay, right?"

Daddy turned away so I couldn't see his face. I felt my stomach sink. He whispered, "I hope so, champ. I really do."

Do you hope that too?

Wishing for a better tomorrow,

A Girl Having a Hard Time with Today

Dear the Man Upstairs,

I realized that Jeanette is named after her dead grandmother, Jenna. (Jenna sounds kind of like Jen, but I try not to think about that.) Everything makes sense now because the only Jeanette I know is an old lady who likes to make sandwiches with Grandma Jen when they feed the hungry at their church. Momo said during a playdate last afternoon that "Jeanette" is the kind of name for a princess in love or a person in a novel who exists only to be a backdrop for the main character's love. I asked Momo what kind of person a "Momo" is. She said that "Momo" is the name of the best friend who serves to parallel the heroine's love and highlight the ways in which the protagonist is her own person.

I asked Momo if people with her name ever got their own stories, and she said, "Maybe, but not in this one." I asked her which one, and she said the one with me and Sean Hanner. I said me and Stupid Sean were never getting together, and she said we would hold hands before my next birthday. I don't know, I think boys have cooties.

After that playdate, I went home to go learn more about my new family that I don't like. Jeanette keeps on showing me YouTube videos of the Victoria's Secret models and talking about how pretty they are, and they really are all that. They're the kind of women other girls look to and kinda hate in that weird place deep inside us no one talks about but everyone has. Even so, I told Jeanette the Victoria's Secret fashion show was immodest because grown women were wearing their underwear in public. She told me to not be such a big baby.

She was saying that when she was a grown-up, she was going to walk in the fashion show. Then she gave me this look up and down, pursed her lips, and said, "Well, what are you going to do with *your* life?"

I thought about if for a second. "I'm going to do something useful, like maybe run a camp to help elementary schoolers with internet and technology addiction."

Jeanette straight up lost it laughing and responded, "What kind of lame interest is that?"

I laughed on the inside because she didn't realize that I meant that she was someone who might benefit from that kind of camp. Instead I said, "I was being sarcastic."

Jeanette said, "Oh, okay. You're just bad at sarcasm then."

I said in a deadpan, "I try."

Jeanette looked really confused. "What?"

I drew out the word. "Sar-ca-sm."

Her eyes widened in understanding. "Oooh." (If there's one thing I've learned from Daddy and Grandma Jen, it's sarcasm. I didn't really get it until this year, but I can learn.) Well, then, back to beautiful people, I just feel like life is easier for them. Jeanette isn't exactly a beautiful girl, but my friend Nina is really, really pretty. Like she has the eyes that hold the entire sky and the ocean and this little upturned nose and super light brown hair with streaks of gold. And the truth is that she can get away with a bit more than me in school. When I was in Mr. Odber's class, if she ever did something wrong, she could just make this shrug and hold her eyes real big and then Mr. Odber would say she didn't mean it. She would agree, and that was enough for everyone. I love Nina to death, and she doesn't always realize just how pretty she is. But sometimes it's hard not to be a little bit jealous.

I think that maybe Jeanette is a bit jealous of me because she said that if I was an Olympic hopeful, I was probably pretty dumb. She was all like, "I bet I can complete more multiplication than you can in five minutes."

I know I'm pretty good at multiplication but bragging about how smart you are is a no-no, so I said, "Yeah, you're probably right."

She challenged me: "Let's have a multiplication competition."

I shook my head. "Let's not and say you won."

She was all like, "So, you admit it then, I'm smarter than you?"

I said, "Not really, but sure. Whatever floats your boat." (By the way, that's a weird saying. Could anything other than water float my boat? Apparently, light corn syrup might work, at least that's what Daddy says.) I think that if Jeanette were more like Samantha, I might have a harder time with her, but Samantha says things that hurt my feelings, and Jeanette just wants to be cool.

When I said that we could just say she was smarter than me, she got really upset. She was like, "Why won't you even try?"

"Because I don't really have anything to prove. I told you I was good at swimming, but I don't need to be smarter than you. We can say you won. Congrats."

Mommy was in the kitchen, and I could tell she was proud of my answer. She gave me a quick thumbs-up and a wink.

Well, then Jeanette said, "But it's no fun unless I know for sure that I'm smarter."

I replied, "If you find it fun to be smarter than other people, you should go bother Ellie-An. She's way more fun than me. She can't even read."

Sincerely,

Miss W

Dear the Man Upstairs,

The other family is leaving on Monday (it's Friday) and thus Jeanette decided it was time for us to have that swim race. I was very excited. I don't get a lot of wins in my life that are as gratifying as the kind of win that I can get against someone who so much wants me to lose. If I ever do really well in life, I'm going to come back to Nelson Elementary and find Ms. Langies and tell her that she was wrong to think that one day I would be a nobody, because then I will be a somebody, and I will tell her that from my somebody position.

The day went something like this: Beatrice offers to drive Jeanette and me in her rental BMW to the YMCA pool because I guess she feels bad that Mommy is always the one taking care of the two of us. It feels like she just now realized it might look bad if she didn't once offer to be the on-deck adult the whole time she was here. Plus, Jeanette just about begged her to come so that way she could make sure my mom didn't somehow magically help me cheat. (That's her excuse now for everything—someone helped me cheat or something like that.)

In the locker room, we get changed, and I get into my one-piece black speedo with red stripes on the sides, and she gets into this tiny, frilled, blue and white polka-dotted bikini. I look at her and say, "I've got a spare suit in my swim bag if you want one."

She looks me up and down and bursts out laughing. "I'd never wear anything as ugly as that. I'd rather be caught dead."

I don't know if that kind of a comment would normally make me feel bad, but this is *swimming,* and Jeanette knows nothing about swimming. So I said, "Then it's your loss, cuz I don't see how you're getting anywhere in that thing."

Jeanette said, "I can still swim in this, and bonus, the lifeguard is cute."

I privately think that the lifeguard is too old to be cute, but Jeanette and I are different people. We go out into the pool, and she says we're just gonna swim one lap to the end.

I ask, "What stroke?"

She says, "Any stroke."

Beatrice stands on the opposite end of the pool and counts down. "Three, two, one, go!" Except Jeanette pushes off at "three."

I stay on the wall until "go" because I figure it won't be much fun if I beat her without a bit of an extra challenge.

When I push off, I am like a bullet, doing my full body waggle under the water with my hands straight in front of my head, for maybe a third of the lap. I come up for my first breath, already ahead of Jeanette, my hand a windmill, my legs kicking repeating again and again. I'd practiced just the day before, so I was ready and willing and moving like Quicksilver from X-Men. I had one hand on the wall before Jeanette was halfway done with the lap. She sees me there and kind of gives up and does this doggy paddle the rest of the way. And you know what she says?

She says, "You pushed off early."

And so you know what I say? "You know what happened, and you'll have to live with that."

She scoffs. "Yeah, and I know you cheated."

But then Beatrice says, "Girls, girls, I took a video with my phone!"

We lean over and try not to drip on the screen as we watch the video, and lo and behold, bam! Jeanette pushes off early. She blushes pink and then she says, "Well, it wasn't fair. I'm in this darn bikini."

Sincerely,

Miss W, the Best Swimmer in *Both* Her Families

PART IV

QUEEN

Dear the Man Upstairs,

It's kind of too bad that right after I beat Jeanette, she went away. The other family has just gotten back in their airplane and flown back to wherever sinkhole they came from. It's weirdly empty here now. Grandma Jen and Lacey are keeping in touch, and Beatrice told Mommy she thinks I'm great. That was nice.

Not everything is nice. Grandma Jen is getting another tumor removal surgery tomorrow. She is definitely super nervous. I mean I would be, too, if I were her. I'm not her, and I'm *still* nervous. But I know she's strong enough to make it okay. The doctors are going to go into her breast and remove a bunch of it, and that's enough to freak anyone out. But Grandma Jen is handling it as well as anyone can, I guess.

Daddy is not handling it well. Daddy is getting even more nervous than Grandma Jen, which is just perfectly ridiculous. He's not the one with a bunch of breast rocks that are about to be cut out of his chest.

Like this morning, I'm making some pancakes for breakfast to be nice to Mommy because she's stressed, and she does a lot of nice things for me, and I can make pancakes. Then I look over and Daddy's pouring orange juice all over the counter and then he sees it and he says, "Sh**!" (a bad word) and then he starts cleaning it up.

And then he looks at me and says, "This friggin' orange juice just had to pick today to spill, you know?" I didn't know what to say, so I nodded.

As he's cleaning, he starts to wipe his eyes, and he says, "God, why is it all happening today?"

And I say, "I don't know, Daddy. Maybe the juice just wanted to be with the counter."

"Well, maybe I just wanted it to stay in the carton, you know? Where it's supposed to be, with all its other orange juice friends. Maybe I just wanted to stay where it was, you know, safe and healthy."

I say, "The orange juice is going to be okay, Daddy."

He says, "I don't want to have to let it go."

I say, "It's better than spilling Ellie-An."

Daddy says, "Yeah. Thank God it isn't one of you."

And then he starts crying for real with big dripping tears and hugs me real tight. "But I wish like heck it wasn't her, either."

Then I started crying, and I said, "But she's gonna be okay, right, Daddy?"

Daddy said, "I hope so, champ, I hope so." And we just stood there, arms around each other, a little bit of orange juice still dripping off our brand-new counters, a little flash of Mommy's laptop from the open-doored office reflecting in the orange juice teardrop, looking for all the world like a firework.

Sincerely,
A Crying Miss W

Dear the Man Upstairs,
Mommy cleaned up the orange juice. I went to school. Fifth grade is hard. I can't stop thinking about Grandma Jen

and tumors. Mr. Odber has been trying his best to be nicer to me because Mommy sent out an email telling all my teachers about what's going on, and Dr. Keaty has been there for me in all our sessions. Sometimes we don't even talk about strategies and just talk about how scared I am for Grandma Jen. Ms. Pepper gave me a hug the other day, and Samantha asked why I needed a hug, and then I said my grandma was in the hospital.

I thought Samantha would say something nasty, and it looked for a second like maybe she would, but then she seemed to really *hear* what I had just said, and she looked at me with these big brown wide eyes and said, "I'm sorry."

I looked back at her with even wider eyes. "Thank you."

I didn't even want to go to school at all, but a girl has got to go to school to avoid an arranged marriage in an autocratic governed country, at least that's what Grandma Jen told me to make me come this morning. She yelled at me over Skype from her hospital bed. Grandpa Q was sleeping next to her because he gets to be with her for medical care all the time now that they're engaged.

I didn't know what autocratic meant, but I used Daddy's phone to look it up. An autocrat is a ruler with absolute power. I've decided my new goal in life is no longer to become a teenager—that'll happen quite easily in three years almost exactly—but I would like to become an autocrat. America seems too big for me to rule effectively, but I was thinking I could make Puerto Rico a state because they deserve to be one, at least that's what Maria always says. She's a seventh-grade swim star and very smart. Then America would have fifty-one states, and everyone would freak out. They'd be all like, "We need to have the same flag with just fifty stars, whatever shall we do?"

Then I would come in and be the hero. "Don't worry! I'll take Alaska. Or even Hawaii."

They'd probably say, "Take Alaska," because there aren't that many people living there. And then boom! I'd be an autocrat.

However, there is oil in Alaska, which is why Aunt Tamara (Mommy's sister) gets to have no income tax and is paid to live there because Alaska makes so much money. (Stupid Sean Hanner was Alaska in international week.) So I could use Alaskan oil to become a rich country, and then I would invest in superpowered solar energy because anyone who has ever gone skiing knows that snow is blinding, so maybe I could have panels that absorb energy both from the sun and its reflection. This new technology would clean up the world, plus I would require people to only work four days a week so they'd never get tired, and schools would spend much less time on homework, plus instead of lockers, people would have closets at schools, and nice showers for after PE. And also, cancer would be illegal in my country.

But you know, now that I think about it, I don't really want to be an autocrat. I'm not that big into ruling other people. I know how much it hurts to have other people think they know better than you all the time and not be able to make the choices you want to make. No one thought to ask *me* how I felt about the medications except for Dr. Keaty and Grandma Jen, sometimes.

Do you like to think of yourself as an autocrat?

I've known for a while now a little more about you than I've been letting on. Like when I first started writing these letters over a year ago, I just thought you were my grandma's friend. But I know now that you are not just some weird guy living above our apartment, talking off and on to Grandma

Jen. I know that "the Man Upstairs" is a name for God. And I'm not stupid. Not like freaking Jeanette thought I was, and not like Ms. Langies thought either. For a girl of my age, all ten years of them, I am decently smart. And so I know that you, the person writing me back, are probably not God.

I wasn't really planning on ever bringing this up because I really like talking to you and telling you about my life and getting your responses back and hearing your words and looking them up. Even if I am smart, I am only ten and all, and I like everything else about these letters, too—and you get the point. So I guess I'm writing this to you for two reasons.

The first is that you haven't written me back since the thing with Jeanette and even then, all your letters have been super short, and I wanted to shock you into writing something. Like I mean, come on, dude, it's a hard time in my life right now, and I could really use some dictionary difficult words right about now. Grandma Jen always says learning replaces yearning if you let the newness seep in with the sadness. I don't understand the whole thing, but I bet if you gave me some good old hard-to-understand wisdom, I might make a better sense of the world, of Grandma's saying, and of my sadness.

I guess the second reason I'm writing this right now is because I want you to know that whoever you may be, you can tell me, and then I'll tell you who I really am—provided you're not some creepy sicko trying to kill me, or even worse, marry me. (I guess the worst-worst would be if you were trying to marry Ellie-An. If you were, I'd have to kill you.) But anyways, I still care about you even though I'm pretty sure you are not God. I don't really mind because you've still been a good friend to me.

Also, I lied. I'm really writing this letter for three reasons and this last one is the most important. I'm ten years old, and I am not stupid. I know that God doesn't write letters to fifth graders just because they are sad and all. God probably doesn't write letters at all, and God may not even exist. But I am still only ten, and maybe I want you to be God. I mean, who doesn't want to be special that way, you feel? Could you imagine if I went up to little Yvette Guiteau and was all like, "Guess what, while you were making bread, I was talking to God," you know?

But more than any of that, and I don't really care about the bragging, maybe just a little, I just want you to be God. I've never asked anything of you before or talked about what I knew because I've never really wanted anything.

If you, "My Man Upstairs," really are God, can you make Grandma Jen get better? And soon, too, better and soon. Please help her get strong enough that she can swing her ugly yellow umbrella like there's no tomorrow. It seems just big enough that she might go flying up any moment as soon as she's done whapping Dad. I'd give just about anything right now to see that.

Sincerely,

A Girl Hoping for a Miracle, Miss W

PS

Please write me back soon.

Dear "Miss W,"

Hello! This is not the Man Upstairs. I'd say I am his friend, but I'm not sure he would agree with me. I'm more like a student. I got your letter to him, and let me start by saying that he really does care about you. The Man Upstairs is more God than anyone I know. I guess I'm saying that on this Earth, we all carry a bit of God and a bit of sky, but the person writing

you back, they are all God, and they carry not just the sky but
also the sun, so I can't say outright that they are God, but I will
say outright that they are far more than just a man.
Sincerely,
A Man of God

Dear Man of God,

So, are you a student like me then? I'm a student. Did you ever have Mrs. N? She's a great teacher, and I trust her. If you're a student, do you think you'd be able to help Grandma Jen? Daddy says that sometimes medical students can still be great doctors. Even if you can't help her get better, will you please at least try?

- Miss W

Dear "Miss W,"
I did not have Mrs. N because I am not a school student.
I am afraid that only the Man Upstairs can help your grand-
mother right now.
-Man Of God

Dear Man of God,

If you are a not a school student, and you can't help Grandma Jen, then you are a stranger, which is dangerous! Stranger Danger! I am scared and must report you to my mother.

- Miss W

Dear "Miss W"
I am not a stranger. I'm a friend of a friend; that means
we're friends.
-Man Of God

Dear Man of God,

Friend of Friend = stranger = my death = must lose contact and contact trusted adult.

- Miss W

Dear Miss W,

Hello again. It's me, the Man Upstairs. I am sorry for taking so long to reply to your letters. I've been a bit busy these last several weeks. It will be springtime soon, and the flowers will bloom once more.

You asked me who I am. I suppose we've been friends long enough I can give you some kind of answer. I am not like Santa Claus or the Tooth Fairy. I am not a fairy tale meant to capture the attention of children and convince them to brush their teeth and be good, for goodness' sake. There are plenty of adults who talk to me just as you, all ten years of you, talk to me.

Children often look to God as an all-powerful entity. Growing up means learning that reality is sometimes filled with things that are hard and unfair. Not every story has a happy ending. That doesn't mean those stories aren't worth reading or living.

I cannot promise you that Grandma Jen will be okay. I can help her have strength to get through what she needs to get through. I can give her faith. I can give her some help on her journey, but I cannot change her destination.

That's all I can do for you, as well. This world is filled with sickness and sadness, but it is also filled with brilliant people who find medicine and families who feel boundless joy. All I can tell you, Miss W, is that these last fifteen months talking with you have made each and every day of my life so much brighter. You are strong. If you ever need someone to lean on, I am here for you in spirit.

It may be that in a long time from now, you will look back at these hard days and realize that you grew into an even more empathetic and compassionate person because of them. As your father often says, "What doesn't kill you makes you stronger." He's a good man, your father.

One day, you may look back at the beautiful person you have become and think that you would still trade all the gifts you received from these challenging days in a heartbeat for your grandmother's health. That's perfectly normal. Still, I think that humans grow because things are hard. It's how you grow from things that are hard, and not how you enjoy things that are easy, that prove you are made in the image of God.

Love,
the Man Upstairs

Dear the Man Upstairs,

It sounds like we are both going through a hard time, but you have fancier words to describe your problems. I don't know if you really are God, but it clearly matters more to you than it does to me, so I'll let you have it. (I don't like that you won't tell me who you are, but I won't tell you who I am, so maybe that's fair.)

I have good news! Grandma Jen is getting strong enough that they released her from the hospital. I went with Mommy to the store, and we bought ice cream to celebrate. We all know that ice cream and Grandma Jen are basically in a symbiotic relationship: you can't have one without the other.

But in an unexpected turn of events, Grandma Jen came home from the hospital and said that she did not want any ice cream at all. She said, "Oh, not tonight, but maybe later." (I'm worried. She's never said no to ice cream, ever. She ate five-year-old ice cream back when she lived in her tiny studio apartment that she found buried behind four-year-old pizza she was never going to eat. So, I don't think being back from the hospital means she's healthy, and that has me worried.)

She wasted no time from coming home to tell Daddy that she loved him, Mommy that the house "looks nice, dear," Ellie-An got a kiss, and Grandma Jen just about showered me with praise on my dealing with a hard spot and on growing into myself because of it.

I told Grandma Jen that she'd really been the one in the hard spot, and she said that tough is tough no matter how tough the tough is. I think I catch the drift of what she is saying but it's hard to know for certain.

The only thing I know for certain is that I love her, and she loves me.

Sincerely,

Miss W, a Worried and Relieved Fifth Grader

Dear the Man Upstairs,

Something great about having made friends with Mon is that the two of us can always cheer each other on before a big meet. Like this last one, we were both trying to one up one another in our supportiveness.

I shouted at him, "You're the best!"

He shouted back, "No, you're the best!"

I said, "You're going to kill it out there."

He responded, "You've already killed it before. Of course, you're gonna murder everyone else today."

Then Amandine, a kind of mean seventh grader with very dark hair, groaned and said, "I'm gonna murder either both of you or myself if y'all don't shut up."

This seemed kind of funny, so we laughed with each other, which really helped to get rid of all the nerves that build up before a competition.

My goodness, sometimes I feel like the little butterflies in my stomach are going to eat me alive and never let me back into the world again. But when I'm talking to Mon, they all just fly away, and by the time I need to get in the pool and swim like there's no weight on top of me, no people behind me, just my legs, my arms, and my speed of light. Winning gold is just a plus of getting to be in the water.

Grandma Jen is getting stronger day by day, and the doctors think there's a good chance she'll go into remission by the summer. She was able to come to the swim meet and congratulate Mon and me and laugh with Coach Summers.

Because Grandma Jen is doing better (but not better enough for ice cream), Mommy and I took her dress shopping for her wedding today. We went to a bridal store, but Grandma Jen wasn't even sure she wanted to wear a whole big gown again because she'd already done that once. She said, "I have half a mind to wear jeans and a polo shirt and call it a day."

Daddy thought that Grandma Jen should just wear a simple dress, not like a big bridal one, and Mommy said, "Jen, you should at least try some real gowns."

That's why we ended up in a real bridal store, and Grandma Jen was hysterical the whole time. It was a sight to see. The first dress she tried on looked like a nightgown and she said, "I am now the bride of dreams."

Then she came out in one that was covered in lace, did a twirl, and said, "Lacey, dear, I wore this for you." Lacey and Beatrice are Mr. Bennet's daughters, and I laughed a lot at that one. I don't really like either of them, but I guess I like Lacey better than Beatrice.

Grandma Jen started nitpicking everything about all of the dresses. "This one is too long," she would complain, or she would say, "This one pearl doesn't shine as brightly as the rest of them. Poor little pearl."

Mommy rolled her eyes after each of the comments and muttered, "It's like house-hunting all over again."

The shop lady with her too-tight bun kept getting more and more annoyed until finally she said, "Just pick something already! You're too old for all these designs, anyways!"

Grandma Jen looked up sharply at the shop lady at that. "Ah, well in that case, I best take my business elsewhere." Grandma Jen started to leave but Mommy was glaring daggers.

"What?" she yelled at the shop lady. "You think only young people deserve to feel pretty at their wedding? You think you can talk to someone that way? You should be ashamed of yourself!"

I started pulling at mom's hand, but she shook me off.

"And so should your mother! She should be ashamed of herself to have raised a daughter like you!"

The shop lady gave Mommy a flat, unimpressed glare.

"Come on, Karen, we can leave a bad review on the Yelp, and on the Google, too!"

Mommy shook her head angrily and looked at the person helping us. "Young lady, what is your name?"

"Ashley," the girl said. "It's on my nameplate."

"Don't you take that tone with me, young lady," Mommy said. "Get me your manager."

The girl did not move.

"I can contact them myself, and then things will go much worse for you," Mommy promised.

The girl disappeared into the back storeroom. Grandma Jen was staring at Mommy like she had never seen her before.

"Okay," Mommy said to me. "Sweetie, I want you to start crying." She paused and then said, "And you too, Mom. Give us some tears."

I'm terrible at fake crying, so I just made this weird face that kinda looks like I'm trying to get poop out, and Mommy said, "Never mind, just look sad." That, I can do.

In the meantime, Grandma Jen's eyes actually started to water, and then she started crying for real with great hiccupping sobs.

Mommy said, "That's great and realistic but you should tone them down a little bit."

Grandma Jen hit Mommy's arm. "I'm not crying because you told me to, you dolt. I'm crying because that's the first time you've ever called me 'Mom.'"

"No, it wasn't." Mommy pursed her lips and looked up to the right as though searching for the rising sun. "Well, it might have been." Then Mommy started crying, and Grandma Jen was crying too, and by the time the manager came out, the two of them were a mess, both sobbing and holding each other's shoulders, their tear-streaked cheeks close as can be and their foreheads resting together.

The manager said, "What happened?"

Seeing the state of the adults, I took matters into my own hands. "The shop lady, Ashley, I think was her name, called my grandmother too old for any of the dress designs. It hurt her feelings, and you know every girl deserves to feel beautiful at her wedding."

The shop manager looked down at me, clearly somewhat confused. "You are absolutely correct. I apologize on Ashley's behalf. We would be delighted to offer your grandmother her dress at a twenty percent discount."

Grandma Jen wiped her face and turned to the manager with bloodshot eyes. "I shall be taking my business elsewhere. She wasn't wrong. This shop *is* too young for me."

She and Mommy began to walk out together, arms around one another's shoulders. I was holding Grandma Jen's hand. As we got near the exit, Grandma Jen yelled, "But you should know that I am leaving you a bad review on the Yelp!"

Mommy whispered, "It's just 'Yelp,' Mom. Not 'the Yelp.'"

Grandma Jen copied Mom in a baby voice, "It's just Yelp, Mom." Then she said, more seriously, "Is 'the Google' wrong, too?"

Mommy nodded.

Grandma Jen sniffed. "Children ought to know that their parents are always right. If I say it's 'the Yelp,' than 'the Yelp' it is."

(I didn't tell her the world doesn't work that way.)

After the whole wedding dress kerfuffle, we went home and sat at the kitchen table. (Mommy texted Daddy to get out of the house and hang out with Ellie-An.) I decided that we were hungry and got out crackers and cheese, but then it turned out that I was the only hungry person and the little plate of cheese and crackers slowly disappeared into my mouth as Grandma Jen sipped her tea and Mommy stared out the soft blue draped window. Grandma Jen put her fist on the table.

"Well, I am old, there's no escaping it." Mommy started to say something along the lines of "you're young in spirit," and I started to say, "age is just a social construct," to which Grandma Jen replied, "We will come back to that later." And she just straight up shushed Mommy.

Grandma Jen continued, "I am old. That's okay. I don't want to be young again."

Mommy shrugged. "Alright. So what?"

Grandma Jen winked at me. "I am proud of being old because it means that I get to have a son, and this little angel, my granddaughter." Grandma Jen squeezed me real tight. I squeezed back.

Mommy said, "Okay," again.

So then Grandma Jen said, "And I am proud of my daughter-in-law too. You know, I always wanted a daughter."

Mommy said, her voice strong and firm, "Thank you."

"You're welcome. Look, Karen, the truth is I don't want to have a wedding without acknowledging the beautiful family I have now and..." Grandma Jen looked down at her hands.

Mommy said, "What are you trying to say?"

"I guess, what I'm trying to say. Karen, is, ah, well, shiz. To heck with this."

Mommy said, "To heck with what, Mom?" And I used all my self-control to not tell them they were poisoning my future with their foul language.

"I've always said I won't mince words, so I'll just come out and say it." Grandma Jen paused and took a deep breath. "Would you plan my wedding, Karen? You know, and help me find a dress, too?"

Mommy stared at Grandma Jen like she had two heads. Grandma Jen kept talking.

"It's just that in the store you stood up for me, and Dr. Keaty called me up the other day, or the other month, you know after the whole medication debate, and she made me see your side of things. You've done such a great job with the house, and all, and I was just thinking I couldn't think of anyone better to... Well, I have no head for these things. You know, I married a carpenter the first time around, and Claude just did everything, and—"

Mommy interrupted Grandma Jen to hug her real tight. "Of course. I would be honored."

Grandma Jen patted Mommy's head awkwardly. "Just don't go now and get a big, inflated ego. It's big enough as it is."

"I love you too, Mom," Mommy said.

"Well, now, I never said that I loved you," Grandma Jen said.

"But you do," I said.

Grandma Jen made eye contact with me. I winked. She smiled down at Mommy. "I suppose I do."

I don't think I've ever smiled so big.

Sincerely,

Miss W, the Granddaughter of the Bride

Dear the Man Upstairs,

Mon told me during swim team that he found Momo's email by looking at my contacts, sent her a letter, and now he's taking her to the school dance.

I said, "What dance?" and then I paused and was like, "What? Why didn't you tell me this earlier?"

Mon shrugged in the water and then sniffed. "It would've sucked if she said no. But she didn't, and now I'm telling you."

In school the next day, we learned all about the fifth-grade dance at Nelson Elementary school from Mr. Odber. He said, "You can invite guests from other schools, but only if they are in the same grade."

That made Pierce upset because apparently he has a girl-friend in sixth grade, but he'll survive.

Momo told me during lunch that Mon asked her out over the weekend, and she's going with him to the dance. Nina said that *she's* going to ask Alex to the dance because she can.

She asked me if I thought anyone was cute, and I said, "I don't think I'm into anyone."

Momo waggled her eyebrows. "Not even Sean Hanner?"

Sean Hanner isn't so bad, really. He stood up to Ms. Langies for me. But, "I call him 'Stupid Sean Hanner' in my head."

Momo laughed. Nina said, "He's not dumb."

I guess Sean Hanner wasn't too far away, because when I looked over at him, he seemed kinda dead. He walked out to the playground. I followed him because he looked sad, and I felt like I had been mean to him accidentally.

We sat next to each other on the swing set. I said, "What's wrong?" and he didn't say anything for a little while.

Finally, he said, "I'm not stupid, you know that? I never liked you anyways. You used to throw slugs at me."

The words "I never liked you, anyways," started rattling around in my head like a bobby pin in a washing machine, going round and round and making this terrible crunching noise. I felt heat rising in my cheeks and a pressure behind my eyes. "I never liked you either!" I yelled. "That's why I threw slugs at you. You *are* stupid!"

Sitting on the swings suddenly felt like I was being trapped, and I rushed to my feet and started to leave but Stupid Sean Hanner grabbed my wrist and said, "Not as stupid as you are!"

I kept my back to him and said, "Oh, yeah, why? Because I need help sometimes, huh? Because you think that just because things go easily for you all the time and you don't get sent to the office every other week, you're smarter than me? Is that it?" I stopped, breathing heavily. I didn't even know why I said all of that.

Sean Hanner looked more and more angry over the course of my whole speech. "Of course not!" he exploded. "If I felt that way, I would have never stood up for you. How stupid can you get? I like you, Miss W, okay? So don't go around calling me stupid because you assume I'm judging you. I'm really not."

So then I stopped facing away from him and turned around. His hand was still holding my wrist.

"What?" I asked.

Sean Hanner looked down out the ground. "I said, 'I like you.'"

"Oh," I said. For once in my life, there was nothing going on in my head. It was like my thoughts had been shocked silent.

"I was going to ask you to the dance, but I guess you don't like me very much, so it doesn't matter."

I jerked my hand free from his wrist and then entwined our fingers together. He looked up at me. "I don't really think you're stupid. I just found you annoying when we were younger, I guess. I didn't like our family picnics. I think if you'd asked me today to the dance, I would have said yes. But then you said you never liked me anyways."

"I lied." Sean Hanner put his free hand through his sandy hair. "I've liked you since second grade when you bounced up and down during my guitar solo." I remembered that, in a vague kind of way. We were family friends then in the uncomplicated way little kids are friends, and he was playing guitar for grandparents' day, and I liked the music so much I couldn't help myself. Everyone else looked at me like I was a weirdo, but Sean had given me this bright grin with two missing front teeth when he was done.

I said, "I think I've liked you since then too. Or maybe since the first slug."

He stood up, so we were eye to eye, but didn't let go of my hand. His face had turned brighter red than the firetruck I used to play with.

"Would you go to the dance with me?" he asked.

I leaned forward and gave him a surprise hug. "Yes. Yes, I will."

He hugged me back. He's just a little bit taller than me now, and he smells like fresh grass.

"Can we be boyfriend and girlfriend?" he asked me.

I thought about this, and then about poor Anna from *Frozen*. "No. Not yet."

And then you will never get what he said, what this boy said, what this dreamy Sean Hanner said. "Okay. You let me know when. I'll be waiting." He walked me home.

Best,

Miss W, a Girl with a Date to the Dance

Dear the Man Upstairs,

Jeanette, Beatrice, and Lacey (but not her husband because he couldn't miss any days of medical school) all came in a few days ago for the wedding. Jeanette is being obnoxious, as usual, but I didn't care. I had a swim meet coming up in Chicago, and Mon was very excited because that's where his dad and older brother live, and they'd never seen him compete before.

I went dress shopping with Nina yesterday because both of us are going to the wedding, and we got our dance dresses at the same time. Momo isn't coming to the wedding because she isn't a family friend, and neither is Alex. The Hanners are totally coming because we've been family friends with them since forever. I really hope Sean Hanner wears a suit because if he did, I bet he would look stupid cute.

Nina got a black dress, and she said she hoped other people will wear the same color so that she can do it better. I said that she was kinda competitive all of a sudden, and she said that she had decided to try out being competitive to see if she liked it. I said as long as she didn't compete with me, I was fine. Nina said, "I would never compete with you. Especially not when you are wearing that dress." My dress is green and billows in the breeze.

When I got back home, Jeanette desperately wanted to see my dress, so I went and put it on, and then she saw me and said, "Hmph." She immediately asked her mom to go out and get another dress. Girls like her are weird.

My swim meet was literally the day before the wedding, so obviously I went to Chicago with Mon and everyone. My family straight-up packed themselves into a tiny old minivan borrowed from Nina's mom and drove up to watch. Even Jeanette came, because she wanted to "see if Miss W really is all that."

Unlike most meets where Mon and I just joke off with one another before the competition, today we were super focused. I gave a "you're a superstar," to Mon, and he gave me a "you're a swim goddess," but the truth was that we were both a little too much in our heads. Bryan was warming up, I was warming up, and Mon was turning into some kind of child-demon in order to get ready for the first meet his dad would ever see.

And then, in the midst of all this pressure, like the three of us kids just holding up the sky, Ellie-An shouts above the noise. She's only five months old, and she can't really talk yet at all, but she gurgled something that I think can be roughly translated to, "I want to swim."

Then she yells very loud nonsense, which can be translated to, "I like water, it makes me happy, and it is beautiful!" I started laughing and so did Mon. It got the nerves right out. The gun goes off. Mon jumps in the pool. His back is straight. His legs are kicking. In no time at all, he's already won.

I won, too, by the way, freestyle four-hundred-meter, and for the first time, I won in backstroke. But Mon was the star today, because when he got out of the water, and got his medals, the boy was dripping rivers onto the ground. And before Grandma Jen could give him her signature hug—she always hugs him even when he's wet—Mon was lifted off the ground and smashed into a hug from his big brother, Ben.

When he was set down on the ground, Ben headlocked Mon and said, "You never told me you were this good, Monty-man. You were holding out on me, huh?"

Mon shrugged. "It's just a hobby." His ears were bright red, like Grandma Jen's nails after she gets them painted, which is a sign that he was embarrassed and pleased. Ben let out this enormous snort, and I was convinced that a bucket of snot was going to come out of his nose, but thankfully, it did not.

"Just a hobby?" Ben shook his head. "No, man, that's a talent. My little brother is freaking talented."

Then Mon's dad came over, and he's this short, bald, and dark-skinned man (almost as short as Mon), and he had this bright smile, and he said, "That's my boy." He shook his head. "How is it that I have two athletic sons and not an athletic bone in my body?"

Mon said, "You should've seen me in Michigan last month. I was a full half-second faster."

His dad said, "I bet you were, but I was just glad to watch you be happy. Man, that look on your face when the gun went off, I can only imagine what this must feel like to you. I'm proud."

Well, then, Mon started crying a little bit and Mommy pulled me away so that they could all have their moment. Mon has put so much pressure on himself, it's a wonder he didn't break down sooner.

Jeanette told me on the ride home that I had looked like a fish in the pool.

"Hey, thanks," I said.

She muttered, "It wasn't a compliment."

Then I said, "But fishes are good at swimming."

And then she said, "If you ever do go to the Olympics, bring me back a medal. Ha-ha, just joking, you won't be able to win anything."

"If I ever got to the Olympics, I'll come home with two golden medals, one for Grandma Jen and one for Ellie-An, and not a single thing for you." And then, because I felt like that was mean and I try to be nice, I said, "But if I ever do an advertisement for a handbag or something, you'll get the first one."

All Jeanette said was, "Hmph," but she did let me get the first scoop of mashed potatoes at dinner, and that means a lot because she likes to steal all the mashed potatoes.

Sincerely,

Miss W, the Friend of a Swim Star

Dear the Man Upstairs,

I went to Grandma Jen and Grandpa Claude's wedding, and it was glorious. This was the toast I gave her right before we ate dinner. I wrote it down ahead of time so I could read it during the wedding.

I said, sitting in a pink dress with a cup in my hands filled with apple juice, "I would like to make a toast to my grandmother. When it first became clear that she was going to get married to Mr. Bennet here, or should I say Grandpa Q now? I don't know, they got married like four seconds ago. Um. Can I start over?"

Some people laughed, but bravely, I pressed on.

"I would like to make a toast to Jennifer Wilson. When it first became clear that she was going to get married to this man over here, the one in the two-piece suit with the blue tie that matches her eyes, I asked if I could give a speech.

"And Mommy said no, because it is unorthodox for such a little kid to get a speech at a wedding. And Grandma Jen said yes, because, as everyone here should know by now, she is unorthodox. She's going to have a red velvet cake for her wedding tonight, the room is decorated in honeysuckles because those are her favorite flowers, and she's wearing a purple dress because, as she told my mom again and again, 'When your hair is white and you wear white, you just look washed out. Plus, I already got married in a white dress before, and heaven knows that I'm not a virgin any longer.'

"I didn't know what a virgin was until about a week ago, but that's really not the point. The point is that for as long as I can remember, my grandmother has never been afraid to do what's right. She wasn't at all afraid to hit Daddy with her yellow umbrella and remind him of how to be a good person, she wasn't afraid to take me out to ice cream when Mommy was baby crazy or help Mommy when poor Mommy had been scammed by an essential oil specialist named Clover. Heck, this gorgeous bride wasn't even afraid of teachers and came into my classroom to help out when a teacher was being particularly mean. She also wasn't afraid to hold me and tell me I was still beautiful when I was feeling like I could never be anything because of my differences.

"My beautiful grandmother has never been anything other than fearless when it comes to doing the right thing, and when she got back a stupid test result, she looked it in the eye and dealt with it. So when she told me she wanted to marry this man in the blue over here, this new grandfather of mine, I knew that he had to be something special and something good. Of course, they had to get married. Because today's bride once told me that the hardest things couples do is have kids, which the two of them both already have, move houses, which she is in the process of doing because they are beginning to live together, and get married, which is what they just did. She's doing the three hardest things couples can do together because my fearless grandmother never backs down from a challenge.

"So I want us all to grab ahold of our metaphorical yellow umbrellas, hit ourselves for not being as cool as she is just yet and not being able to look at our deepest fears straight in the eyes just yet, and raise our glasses in a toast to this magical woman and her newfound magical husband. There has never been anyone anywhere as brave or as loving as Jennifer Wilson. I love you, Grandma Jen, I really do.

"Cheers!"

Mommy told me on the car drive home when I was still in my pink dress and Grandma Jen was with Grandpa Q, "I was wrong. I should have known from the beginning you would give a great speech."

I didn't say anything, just looked out the window at the shining stars that seemed so much like a planetarium and hoped that Grandpa Claude was happy for Grandma Jen, wherever he might be.

Hooray for Weddings,

Miss W, One of Quincey Bennet's New Granddaughters

Dear Miss W,

The wedding was amazing. I am glad to see your grand-mother so happy, and I heard your speech was the highlight of her wedding. Congratulations to you both.

I know that this wedding comes after days of fear and heartbreak, and I am so glad you had a moment of peace. You are growing up, Miss W, and will become even more beautiful in the future than you already are, inside and out. We've been writing letters to one another for almost two years now. Your imagination is quite frankly astonishing. I've always looked forward to hearing from you. You have shown me how to see the world in vivid color, and I am so grateful to have had the chance to see Earth through your eyes.

I do not know if I will be able to keep writing you letters for the rest of your life, but I want you to know that I am endlessly proud of you. That, I promise you, will never change.

With love,
the Man Upstairs

Dear the Man Upstairs,

Thanks for the congratulations! I get that you won't be able to keep writing me letters for the *rest* of my life because that would be crazy. I hope we can keep writing to each other for a long time, though, because you've been one of my best friends for a while now. I actually think that I now have five whole friends, and when I first started writing to you, I only had Nina and Momo and sometimes Sean Hanner. He was the half in my two and a half friends. (Today, I've got you, Nina, Momo, Sean, and Mon.) Since we're friends, we should stay in touch for as long as we can, okay?

Now that the wedding is over and Grandma Jen's moved in with Grandpa Q, I get to stay in her old room. This is perfect because this week, Ellie-An moves into my old room, so now the two of us won't have to share a room, and I won't have to listen to a crying, but cute, baby.

Grandma Jen left behind a bunch of little notes for me everywhere. I still haven't found them all. Most of them just say things like, "I love you," or "You can do anything, but not everything" but some of them are clues. Like one of the last ones I found, a Post-it note stuck underneath the bed, said "Look to your left." So now I've been searching the left side of the room, but I haven't found anything. Grandma Jen told me that in the end, I had to be the one to figure it out myself.

"I'm not giving you any spoilers," she said.

I'll figure out all the clues someday, but in the meantime, Ellie-An has turned six months old! It was her half-birthday, and we all got together and had a party for her. I thought it was a little weird because we don't normally celebrate half-birthdays, but Grandma Jen was stubborn. She said that it was necessary because, "I want to have at least one memory of a birthday with my youngest granddaughter." I thought that it was perfectly ridiculous because Grandma Jen is getting so much better and her memory is just fine, but sometimes people say weird things after weddings.

Of course, Mommy had said there would be no cake for the half-birthday party, but Grandma Jen had said, "No baby of mine gets a birthday without a cake."

Mommy said, "Well, she's my baby, actually."

Grandma Jen had put her finger over Mommy's lips and said, "Shhh. It's okay."

I am a big fan of cake, so I was on Grandma Jen's side. Mommy and Grandma Jen reached a compromise. Ellie-An got half a cupcake, which she couldn't eat because she's a baby-baby, but everyone else also got half a cupcake, and I can eat cupcakes. Then we all looked back at baby photos of Ellie-An, and Grandma Jen had snuck in and added baby pictures of me into the slideshow, and then people kept on being like, "Wait, is that Miss W or Ellie-An," and then only Grandma Jen always knew the answer. She said it was because she knew how we looked the best, but Mommy said it was because Grandma Jen was the one who changed up the slideshow.

Daddy just kept on being impressed with himself for having made such cute babies, and he kept saying, "I must have had pretty good genetics, huh?"

Grandma Jen always replied, "Naturally."

Gammy and Gampa called Ellie-An to congratulate her, but she didn't understand phones and tried to wipe her nose with it. Mommy talked to them for a good long while in her office and came out with red eyes. It was too cold to go to park that afternoon even though it's already March, but then we found an indoor playground, and Mommy reserved a party room, and then this whole class of three- to eight-month-olds from playgroup came, and we got to meet Mommy's friends, and only one of them was not wearing yoga pants, and that one person was a dad. Even so, they were all really nice and the babies were cute.

We all knew that Mommy had found her people, because they all did Pilates and spin classes, drank soup and no cream in their coffee, and were super caring of their babies. Mommy is a little bit a completely different Mommy with Ellie-An than she was with me, but she kept on showing me off to all the other mothers, and at the end of the day she said, "I know it was hard for us a few years ago, but Miss W, I just want you to know that I wouldn't want you to be any other way. I hope

Ellie-An can grow up to be half as good as you." Grandma Jen is great, but she isn't always right about everything. Maybe Pilates and yoga pants aren't so bad, after all.

Sincerely,
Miss W, the Older Sister of a Six-Month-Old Baby

Dear the Man Upstairs,

I went to the dance with Sean. He looked stupid cute, and so did I, so we were pretty stupid together. The truth is that I don't really like loud music, and they were playing the worst music they could possibly find—it was all wub-wub-wub with no words. The two of us decided to go attack the peanut M&M's, and we began throwing them into each other's mouths, and I actually caught five of them, but Sean only caught two. He said it was because I was a bad thrower, but he and I both know the truth.

We decided to go outside because it was so hot, so so hot, in the room with all the middle schoolers. It smelled the way Daddy smells after he goes on a run. The two of us went out to the field and watched our breath make tiny puffs in the air before it was too cold, and we went back inside and leaned our backs against the glass door.

We just talked for a while, first about how the clouds looked like little figs trying to become apples, and then about how weird it was that we'd been in the same class since kindergarten, and then about how one day Sean was going to become a famous guitar player, and I would become a famous swimmer. We could be famous together.

Momo came running down the stairs with Mon. Mon told me, "You have plenty of arms," and had glitter in his hair.

I thought this was a weird thing to say, and I said, "What does that mean?"

He said, "You have enough arms to move your pretty butt and get dancing."

I said, "You have two working legs. Why aren't *you* dancing?"

Momo said, "Because I wanted to come find you. Let's dance together, please?"

And I can't say no to Momo, especially not when she's all dressed up with flowers braided into her hair, so I said, "Okay, Sean, let's go dancing."

I took his hand, and we went back into the room right before they started playing a slow dance song. Sean and I put our hands around each other and swayed to the music. I leaned my head on his shoulder and decided that this must be what it's like to be a grown-up.

After the dance was over, Mommy came to pick me up. Her eyes were red around the edges, and instead of driving fast like normal, she pulled over on the side of the road. She told me to come and get in her lap like I used to do when I was smaller, and she pulled me real close and folded down around me.

"Miss W," she said, and so I said, "Yes, Mommy?"

"Miss W," she said again, "Grandma Jen is in the hospital."

So I said, "Why?"

And then Mommy said, "Because she collapsed. They did some tests, and they just found a tumor in her brain. It's growing fast, and—"

But I interrupted, "And she'll be okay, right? And she's gonna get better because there are doctors who can fix her." And then I felt warm water drip onto my head, and I knew Mommy was crying.

Mommy whispered, "I'm so sorry, baby. They said it's stage four. They said it's time for us to say our goodbyes."

But that's stupid, Man Upstairs, because I don't want to say goodbye.

- Miss W

Dear the Man Upstairs,

Some days you feel like you are underwater, and no matter how hard you kick, you can't figure out which way is up, and so your breath is burning, and you are no longer breathing. You are working so hard but no matter how hard you push it is only getting darker, and colder, and you begin to realize that you will never see the sun again.

And normally when I have those kind of days, I go to Dr. Keaty, and she tells me that making progress is not always linear, but that I am doing a good job. Or, more likely, Mommy tells me to come have a smoothie with her and she takes me to yoga, or Daddy reminds me that what doesn't kill me makes me stronger and tells me to "Come watch that dance thing you like, champ."

But most often, when I'm feeling like the top of my head has dropped to underneath my feet, Grandma Jen will put her arms around my shoulder, yell at someone for the mere heck of it, and take me to try that new flavor of ice cream. Last time, on the drive, she yelled at this goose that had been waddling out in the middle of the road, and she'd said, "Mr. Goose, you dolt, you're going to get run over! Move along, will ya? Shoo," and then she had turned to me shaking her head and said, "Really now, some people."

And you know, I never realized until yesterday that when I grow up, I want to be just the same way. I'm gonna have a big old umbrella, not yellow because that's her thing, and I'm gonna hit my children with it, and shelter my grandchildren with it, and I'm gonna take these knees that used to be black and blue from hiding underneath desks and use them to walk my family to ice cream. And I'm not stupid, I know that people have to die one day. But I guess I always just thought that Grandma Jen would be there to see me with *my* children at least for a little while, and even if she didn't live quite that long, I thought for certain I would see her sitting at my elementary school graduation, wiping away tears she clearly created with eye drops, and then driving me home in the car and complaining about how all of my teachers looked like they were Muppets.

But yesterday, when Mommy took me to see her, I was still in my pretty green dress Grandma Jen had said made me look the most beautiful she's ever seen me just a few hours before. She was lying on a white bed, and she could not open her eyes. The breast cancer had been doing alright with radiation, but then I guess a few weeks ago, they realized it was metastatic, which means that it's spread to other parts of her body. I guess the big problem is that it got to her brain. Grandma Jen went through with the wedding and stopped radiation and came home from the hospital because she wanted her last memories to be happy ones. At least, that's what Daddy told me. He's known this whole time, and so has Grandpa Q and Mommy.

The nurse said Grandma Jen has a fast-growing tumor in her brain, and it just compromised her reticular formation, so she cannot stay awake. I don't know much about brains and reticular formations, but apparently, they don't want to surgically remove the tumor because if they did, Grandma Jen would never be able to wake up. But if they don't, Grandma Jen will never be able to wake up. In general, it looks like Grandma Jen will never be able to wake up. And they said the cancer will probably kill her by the end of the week.

And I know that everyone wants to die in their sleep, so maybe it's not so bad that this is how she's going to go. Maybe she's lucky, maybe she's happy because she was smart and funny and healthy right until the end. But I am not happy, and Grandpa Q is not happy, and Daddy is not happy, and Mommy is not happy. Even though Mommy is trying to keep us all together, we're all crumbling inside, and Ellie-An is too little to understand so she kept reaching for Grandma Jen saying something that sounded like, "Gammy, Gammy, Gammy," but Grandma Jen isn't reaching back.

So, I took Ellie-An and said, "Shh, Grandma's coming," but it's the first lie I've ever told aside from, "Nooo, Mommy, I did not eat that cookie, I don't know how the crumbs got on my mouth."

Mommy and Daddy let me sleep in their bed last night after we went home, which never happens. I've never been allowed to sleep in their bed, and they cuddled me between them all night. I think it was raining inside, or maybe we were all crying, but that just doesn't seem right somehow because we were all too cold to cry. And then Mommy stroked my head and Daddy's, and said, "Baby, it's gonna be alright," but it's not alright, and everybody knows that.

So I'm gonna ask you again, Man Upstairs, are you God? Because if you are, please fix this, please let her get healthy again.

Sincerely,

Miss W, Please Help Us

Dear the Man Upstairs,

Daddy took me fishing today. It was kind of like our last outing before we go and stay by Grandma Jen's side until the end. I feel like we could both kind of hear her saying, "My time will come, but it is NOT today, so move your sorry butts and get doing something." So we had to do something because the Grandma Jen in both of us demanded it.

Daddy took me out onto the water, and at first, we were both just focusing on getting fish, and we were tossing back the flip-flops and soda cans we pulled out of the lake willy-nilly. I guess I decided that this was stupid because there was this huge elephant on the boat neither of us could talk about. I am not the kind of girl who ignores elephants.

I said, "I'm going to miss her," but when a girl is crying all that can come out sometimes is "agjhjathjkathkhjkaaa!"

And then when I looked up, Daddy was crying, too, and I'm pretty sure he was trying to say, "Me too, champ, me too," but all he could manage was, "memem twiioim jkaKakKSdjkHJdhj."

We put our arms around one another and wrapped each other up and sat watching our breath make little clouds in the air and felt all this heat from the two of us get eaten up by the cold air.

We went to get hot chocolate after we got back to shore, and Daddy started crying as soon as he got it. I was reminded of how Grandma Jen watched us shovel snow that one time when she was sipping her hot chocolate, and then I started crying before I decided it was stupid for me to cry. I slapped my face and then I slapped Daddy, and then I said, "Wailing is for baby children, wallowing is for baby sea creatures, and moving on is for human beings!"

Daddy gave me a laugh that sounded a lot like a choked sob and said, "You know you got the words wrong."

I hadn't known, and I decided it didn't matter, so I said, "It's the meaning that matters."

Daddy nodded once, seriously, and then looked at me. I don't know what he saw, but I must have looked pretty sad. I bet my eyes were glassy and my lips were trembling because Daddy said, "It's okay to cry, champ."

That reminded me so much of all those letters I sent to you back in fourth grade when you, the Man Upstairs, told me it was okay to be sad sometimes. I thought about those letters and said, "I know."

When we came home, we both had red-rimmed eyes, and we told Mommy that we had caught the biggest most beautiful fish and then we had let it go because it was going to be happier in the lake. Mommy's eyes got all watery, and I could tell she was going to cry but instead she made this terrible face and swallowed her tears, it seemed.

She said, "Well then, the two of you are my heroes for being so good to the fish. I hope it finds its way to paradise."

Sincerely,

Miss W

Dear the Man Upstairs,

Write me back already! Tell me something, anything! TELL ME THAT IT'S GOING TO BE OKAY. Or tell me that you are okay, or that I am okay, or that this is going to be not okay and that will be okay.

I went to visit Grandma Jen, and I was crying, and I couldn't stop. Grandpa Q was sitting beside Grandma Jen's bed, holding her hand, and Mommy put her hand on his shoulder and told him, "It's going to be okay, Quincey. It's going to be okay."

He shook his head and said, "I've loved once already and lost her. To have loved again and lost again…." He didn't finish. He just kissed Grandma Jen's forehead and pressed his cheek against her cheek.

Mommy said, "There will be others, you know."

Grandpa Q said, "But for me, this is enough. Birds mate for life, you know, and I was lucky enough to find two beautiful women to love for all their lives. Two lifetimes of love is almost more than a man can bear. And I would have been happy with just one, and I thought that maybe this time…"

He couldn't finish, and Mommy didn't press him.

I was still crying but I said, "But, Grandpa Q, it will be alright."

He patted my knee and said, "No, my dear. It will never be alright. It will get easier, but this loss is never going to be alright."

And so I ask you, Man Upstairs, God, or whatever or whoever the heck you are. What kind of world includes death like this in the code? What kind of God lets people like Grandma Jen die and people like criminals live? How is that fair? Why do the bad things always happen to good people? And where are you? Why aren't you talking to me? I NEED you. Tell me it's going to get better, tell me that you are going to get better, or tell me you aren't, just please, please, please, tell me anything at all.

Sincerely,

Miss W

Dear Grandma Jen,

Hi, it's me. Your granddaughter. Not Ellie-An, but I bet you knew that. Um, the nurse said that even though you are asleep, you might still be able to hear me, and so I wanted to talk to you before the end. They say that you're going to die today, just so you know. I think that you would want to know, but don't worry, even though I'm sure that it's very scary. I'll make you smile soon, so you can feel happy at the end. We're all here in this room, too, me, and Daddy, and Mommy, and

Ellie-An, and Grandpa Q, and Uncle Mathias has flown in from California, and we're here right now.

I wanted to say thank you. First. I know that you've been writing letters to me for about two years now as the Man Upstairs. I'm not really sure when I figured it out, but I started wondering about it when you almost knew Grandpa Q was going to propose and the only person I told was the Man Upstairs. And then I knew for sure when you collapsed a few days ago and the letters stopped. I asked Grandpa Q about it, and it turns out that he was the Man of God from the first round of cancer. So there was never any stranger danger to protect against. Don't worry. I'm not angry that you didn't tell me. I needed a friend, and you were everything I needed and more.

The clue you left in your room helped me figure out that you were the person writing me back too. I looked at the left side of every room in our house, and I found a loose floorboard in the kitchen with all my letters to the Man Upstairs in a box underneath. You haven't thrown even one away. That's part of how I know you're ready to go on this next part of your existence. I guess you've known for a little while now that this part was at an end. I didn't know, but I think I'm starting to figure it out.

I think you already know from all my letters how amazing you've been as my grandmother because you're the kind of person who told me to keep my chin up high and grow in my character and all of that other mumbo-jumbo I'm still trying to make sense of. And we got to try every ice cream flavor, so at least there's that. But as the Man Upstairs, you were a constant friend, someone who never judged me and accepted me completely as the person who I was and the person that I am.

In my very first letter to you, I thought that whenever you cried, it rained. It was raining a lot in those first few letters, and I was very worried about you. I just want to tell you right now, that even though it might seem like we're all crying, and even though you are probably worried, that it is just raining, and that the sun is going to come out soon, and that we're all going to look at this big, beautiful rainbow, and know that you helped make it. And I want you to know that you're not alone sitting in the middle of the good and the bad, you are standing in the middle of the world with lots of love, surrounded by your family.

And I want you to know that we all had a chat and decided that we would line your grave with honeysuckles and have a little yellow umbrella on the stone, and you're going to be lying next to Grandpa Claude. And it's going to be such a pretty place, and it's going to be warm, but not too warm, and you're going to be wearing a purple dress in your casket, and we're all going to be singing "Gloria" at your funeral because it's your favorite song even though we know it isn't Christmas or even very appropriate.

I'm going to give you that first gold medal I won, the one that we have a picture of us biting either end, because you are a champion, and you have made me a champion. And, even though you can't tell us, we want you to know we know that you love us, too, and that we can hear you saying it again and again.

We talked it over, and we've decided on what we're going to write for you. It's going to say, "Here lies Jennifer Wilson, beloved mother and grandmother. Now that you've read all about who I am, move your little butt, figure out who you are, and go change the world." We all think that it speaks for itself. So that's it from me. I'm off to change the world. Until we meet each other again, Grandma. Say hello to my little brother for me. I'll see you both on the other side.

Love,
Your Granddaughter

Dear the Man Upstairs,

Hey. When I was a fourth and fifth grader, I wrote you many letters, but they were answered by my grandmother. I'm pretty sure you've met her by now. She died about eight years ago. I just graduated from high school, and I thought I would give this thing another go.

I have a message to her (and you) that I would love to be passed along. It's the least you can do. I'm sure that Grandma Jen's been taking care of you for ages, making sure you're sleeping enough, and treating us humans gently, and that you are working hard and not slacking off.

She told me once that in a few years I might look back on the time she was sick and be grateful for the gifts it gave me. It's been long enough, and now I have a response. To be honest, I did grow. Sure, I cried for the first year or two, but I got stronger, and my friends really supported me, and now Momo, Mon, Sean, Nina, and I are all going on a road trip together before we ship off for college.

Oh, I got into college! I got recruited for swimming, and I'm going to the University of Michigan. I even have a roommate who's on the swim team and we're going to be in the dorms together. The University of Michigan isn't too far from home, and Mom's already planned on driving out to see me at least once a month, because, as she puts it, "I'll go into withdrawal without you." Mom really likes to talk to me now, and maybe that's because I've gotten better at listening to her. Or maybe that's because she's better at being interesting. Or maybe both.

Dad quit his job grant writing and became a teacher. He teaches high school history, and he started making AP US History YouTube tutorials and they've gone viral, and now a lot of his money comes from his YouTube. He's not famous but he's not not famous. And Mom's interior design business is still doing well enough. She has an intern this summer.

And I'm a creative writing major and business minor because my whole life numbers haven't gotten lost in the same way words can, so I like to have a mix of things I learn. Plus between all the swimming, and the growing older, and the meetings with Dr. Keaty, I'm doing pretty well these days. Not to brag, but I'm doing great.

I want you to tell Grandma Jen that I talked about her so much Ellie-An's started writing letters to her. You know Ellie-An is about to be a third grader, and she's around the same age I was when I started writing to you. From all her stories and challenges, you'd think she was grown-up. It's crazy how much life a nine-year-old goes through.

I'm writing her back too, as Grandma Jen. She doesn't know I'm the one writing her back yet, and I do my best to channel my inner Grandma. I keep on telling her that mean girls are character building, and that I love her and am proud of her. I also encourage her to get ice cream with her older sister, and it's become a tradition between the two of us. I take her out to get ice cream, just me and her, every Sunday. And sometimes, whenever she wants to, we'll go buy some honeysuckles and say hello to Grandma Jen.

Oh, and I have a bright pink umbrella now, and I hit Dad with it when he's being a little slow, and I give it to Ellie-An whenever it's raining and she's unprepared, and I even shared it one time with Sean when he was walking me home. He's going to Michigan, too, by the way. Not that you asked, but I answered.

I'm not mailing this to you, Man Upstairs. I'm going to burn it, because I'm pretty sure mail won't reach you if I send it, and you probably already know everything I'm saying if you're real anyways.

Most of all, I just want to tell you and Grandma Jen that my life has gotten better. No more hiding under desks or getting lost for me. I'm finding and found. Grandma Jen told me once that if I could, I would one day trade back everything that made me grow in order to have her healthy. And that's probably true for me, or really, that's definitely true. But she also told me once that growth, more than ease, was in the image of God. And so, the Man Upstairs, I want you to tell her that I'm growing up. I'm growing up in her image, and that's God enough for me.

Love,
Amber Wilson

ACKNOWLEDGMENTS

Writing this book has been a journey and a half. Just three years ago, I was a high school student who had no idea that I would ever finish, let alone publish, a book. I have been so blessed to watch my dreams become a reality. I would like to extend my everlasting gratitude to everyone who has helped me throughout this process. Thank you for proving that not every hero wears a cape.

Here are all the heroes who have been integral to the making of this novel:

Adam H. Tachner, Adele Gershater, Amber and Jeff Rosen, Ana Luisa Davidovits Evans, Andrea and Alan Booth, Andrew Solway, Ariella Radwin, Ashley Caisse Betsy R. Gullickson, Betty Kaufman, Bill and Lisa Kelly, Bob Zeidman, Camden Brito, Carol Tannenwald, Chris Zable, Claire A. Manning, Cliff Swain-Salomon, Dale Pearlman, Darren Kleinberg, David Cleverdon, David Marcus, David and Carol Booth, Deborah Booth, Donald Golden, Edward Gornish, Elise Sprague, Emeri Handler, Enrique Heredia, Eric Koester, Eric Solway, Erika Amemiya, Erika Shapiro, Erin Grace, Esther Hadar and the Rosenfeld family, Frona Kahn, Gabriella Safran, Gabriella Sahyoun, Harry Saal, Heather Silverman,

Isabella Phillips, Isabelle Poux, Janis Popp, John Lewis, Jonathan Manousaridis, Joseph W. Cleverdon, Joshua Booth, Judith Goldkrand, Judith Zeitlin, Judy Kitt, Justin Graham, K. Fitzpatrick and the Bajot Family, Karen Barbara Patou, Kimberly Sprague, Kristen Carlson, Larry Barasch, Laura Tannenwald, Laurie Matzkin, Lewis Warshauer, Lisa Kolbe, Maggie Comstock, Marc Brown, Marc and Julia Itzkowitz, Marcella Bernstein, Mariel Bolhouse, Mark Kelman, Marlene Booth, Mary Cleverdon, Matthew Solway, Melinda Joffe, Beth Jackson, Melody and Alan Solway, Michael Schwartz, Michele Sullum, Michelle Oberman, Mika Illouz, Mike Krigel, Naomi Booth, Natalie Telis, Nina Wouk, Randi Brenowitz, Rita A Koger, Ruth Itzkowitz, Ruthie Caparas, Sally Goodis, Samuel Allen, Samuel Thomas, Sarah Miller, Shaina Hammer, Tamar Hartmayer, Tamika J. Hayes, Tarn Wilson, Tatyana Belova, Wendy Allyn, William Bentkowsky, Yekaterina Prupis, Zan Gerhardt, and Zurisadai Rodriguez

I'd also like to thank the group of beta readers who've supported my campaign and given me feedback on my writing: Judith Klass, Adrian David, Gabriel Williams, Vanessa Thomas, and Antonio Macaggnan.

My team at NDP have my undying appreciation. Thank you Eric Koester, Melody Delgado Lorbeer, and Chelsea Olivia for inspiring me to write and continue to this point.

A special thanks goes out to my siblings. You've both been here for me since day one of my life. I could not have done any of this without you.

Made in United States
Orlando, FL
01 January 2024

41972485R00137